WELCOME
TO THE
FUTURE

For all those new to the world, especially my niece Vivienne and nephew Benjamin. The future is yours to create.
-K.H.

WELCOME
TO THE
FUTURE

WRITTEN BY **KATHRYN HULICK**

ILLUSTRATED BY **MARCIN WOLSKI**

Frances Lincoln
Children's Books

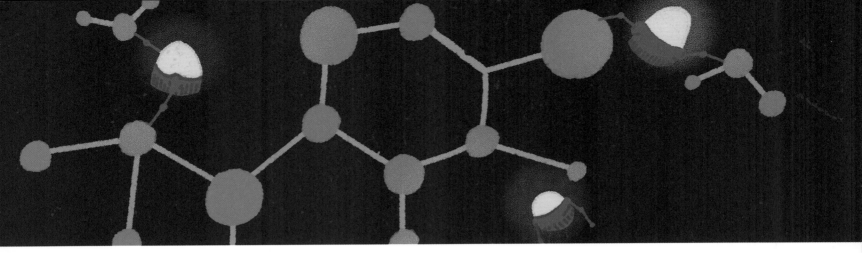

INTRODUCTION

In the future, will we teleport from place to place, keep dinosaurs as pets, live on Mars, or upload our brains to computers? Will we befriend robots or 3D print our dinners?

These are some of the questions we'll explore in this book. Each chapter opens with a vision of a wondrous future that technology might make possible. The challenge for you is to think deeply and carefully. What sort of future do you want for yourself, your family, and your world?

Technology advances at breakneck speed all around us, as scientists and engineers ponder and imagine, tinker and test, program and debug. They are creating the future. Today, cars drive themselves. People control mechanical arms or legs with their minds. Medical engineers print patches of human skin. Things change fast, but the more you learn about what's possible now, the better prepared you'll be for what's possible next year or five years from now.

Beyond that, things get murky. Predicting the future is a tricky business. What actually happens is often even stranger than fiction. Back in the 1950s, people imagined robot servants, space settlements, and flying cars. They didn't imagine that a computer might fit in your pocket, or allow you to instantly connect with anyone, anywhere in the world. Now, we have smart phones, but can't visit Mars on holiday or ask a robot to make a sandwich.

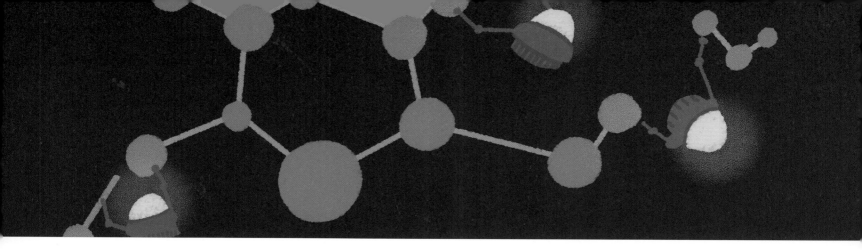

Sometimes, a technical barrier holds back a fantastic technology. One reason we don't have robot servants is that mechanical hands can't yet pick up any kind of object. Other times, money is a barrier. Fusion reactors are ridiculously expensive to build and run, so research in this area has moved slowly.

The final thing to consider is whether something is right or wrong. This is also called ethics. Just because we can do something doesn't mean we should. So far, we haven't been willing to risk people's lives to go to Mars, so we've sent robots instead. Similarly, flying cars could easily exist; we already have helicopters, after all. But flying is trickier than driving and accidents that happen in the air are much more dangerous. Safety is only one of the reasons we should think twice about doing something. The rich and powerful may use new technology to oppress or control others. And new technology may clash with some people's beliefs or values. The voices of all people matter when it comes to choosing our future.

Technology by itself is never simply good or bad. Technology is a tool and it's how people use that tool that matters. For example, someone could use a 3D printer to make weapons. Or they could print homes to replace ones lost in a natural disaster. A mad scientist could some day genetically engineer a monster. But genetic engineering also made it possible to rapidly develop vaccines for COVID-19. We should not fear technology. We should seek to understand it and use it to make the world a better place.

Something may seem impossible today, but there's no stopping human imagination, creativity and willpower. When you know the world you want to live in, you can help create it. Welcome to the future.

CONTENTS

ROBOTS EVERYWHERE

You wake up to the sound of music you've never heard before. "I thought you would like this song," says your personal robot. You're already humming along. "Save it to my favorites," you say.

Your robot is here to wake you and make sure you have everything you need during the day. It brings you clothes to wear and takes away your pajamas to wash them. It suggests some ideas for breakfast, then prepares your food and cleans up when you have finished. Robots also run factories and restaurants. They build roads and houses and fix anything that breaks. They even repair and program themselves. Since people no longer have to work, the government provides everyone with the money they need to live, learn, and pursue whatever hobbies they enjoy. Today, you're practicing with your band.

A self-driving car takes you to band practice. Overhead, drones buzz past, delivering packages and taking away things people no longer need. Robots have made the world a safer and more convenient place. They take care of everything.

People might live life as a never-ending vacation.

It's easy to imagine a world in which mechanical servants care for humans. Wouldn't it be awesome never to wash dishes or fold laundry, ever again? And most people don't want to work long hours at a stressful or dangerous job or do piles of boring homework. If robots could take on any type of work, people might live life as a never-ending vacation. It sounds amazing.

ROOMBAS, DRONES, AND MORE

Will people ever live in a world like that? "I think we will," says Ross Hatton. He's a robotics engineer at Oregon State University. To him, this future seems achievable within our lifetime. Robots are already making people's lives easier. The Roomba and many similar floor-cleaning robots vacuum or mop floors automatically. The company Waymo's self-driving cars have logged over twenty million miles on public roads in 25 different cities. You can buy a drone that will follow you and film you as you bike, skateboard, or snowboard. Robots are even more common in industry. They make things in factories, monitor construction sites, and fetch and deliver items in warehouses and hospitals. Robots even milk cows.

Robots take whatever shape makes sense for their job.

These robots were each designed to perform one specific job. They don't tend to look like the humanoid creatures of science fiction. Instead, they take whatever shape makes sense for their job. The first robot to become widely successful looked like a giant, boxy metal finger. It was called Unimate and its job was to weld car parts together on an assembly line. So what made it a robot and not just another machine? No one had to drive it. Someone could program it, or give it instructions, and then it would follow those instructions on its own. On the Tonight Show in 1966, Unimate knocked a golf ball into a cup, poured a drink and conducted a band.

ROBOT, MAKE ME A SANDWICH!

So if all that was possible in 1966, why don't we have household robots that do all our chores already? Why can't a robot roll into your kitchen and make you a peanut butter sandwich? Let's go through three big problems this robot would face.

The first problem is that human kitchens are built

for human bodies. You can crouch or stand and reach. So the robot would also need to be flexible enough to access places that are down low or up high. You can use your hands to pull open drawers, twist knobs, or undo latches. You can pick up objects without squashing, breaking, or dropping them. It's easy enough to build a robot that opens a specific drawer, twists a specific knob, or picks up a specific object. You just program the robot to perform a sequence of precise motions. The tricky part is building a robot that can notice, reach for, and grasp anything, without being told where or what it is in advance.

Most robots lack a sense of touch.

Picking things up probably seems easy to you. But your brain does a lot of hard work behind the scenes. It calculates where the object is and how far you have to reach to touch it. It figures out how many fingers need to be involved in grasping and where they should go. It adjusts the grip if the object is slippery, or fragile, or very heavy. You practiced reaching and grasping when you were a baby. So now, you don't have to think about any of these things. But a robot does. Plus, most robots lack a sense of touch. "Imagine trying to grab something while wearing big oven mitts," says Michael Gennert, a roboticist at Worcester Polytechnic Institute. That's what grasping is like for most robots.

Engineers are working on soft robot grippers that can touch. They've even designed octopus-style tentacles. But no matter what a robot's hands look like, it needs practice. An artificial intelligence technique called deep learning gives computers and robots the ability to learn from examples (see Chapter 10). The more examples, the better. Ken Goldberg of the University of California, Berkeley has set up a virtual world of around 10,000 virtual 3D objects called Dexterity Network (Dex-Net for short). A robot's software can practice gripping different objects in the virtual world before it picks up anything in the real world. Goldberg's robots can pick up boxes and other simple shapes at a similar speed to a human. But it could take decades or more before robots grasp any object as nimbly as people do.

FINDING YOUR WAY

The second problem is that everyone's kitchen is different. No matter how tidy you are, a roboticist would call your kitchen an unstructured environment. This just means that a robot has no way of knowing ahead of time exactly where to find the fridge, cutlery drawer, pantry, or anything else it might need to make a sandwich. This is a problem for people in unfamiliar kitchens, too. But at least people know where things are likely to be and what everyday objects look like. A robot has no idea.

> No matter how tidy, to a robot, your kitchen is an unstructured environment.

First of all, the robot would need a computer vision system that allows it to recognize a fridge or cupboard no matter the size or color. It would also need to identify objects to avoid crashing into, like walls and chairs. Then it would have to create a map of the room and plan its movements. All of this is already possible, thanks partly to deep learning and other artificial intelligence techniques. Engineers train computer vision software by showing it millions of examples of the objects it needs to recognize or avoid. Through this process, self-driving cars have learned to see and avoid people and other cars in the road.

However, being able to find the fridge and get there without knocking over any chairs is only part of the problem. "You have lots of knowledge about the world when it comes to making a sandwich,"

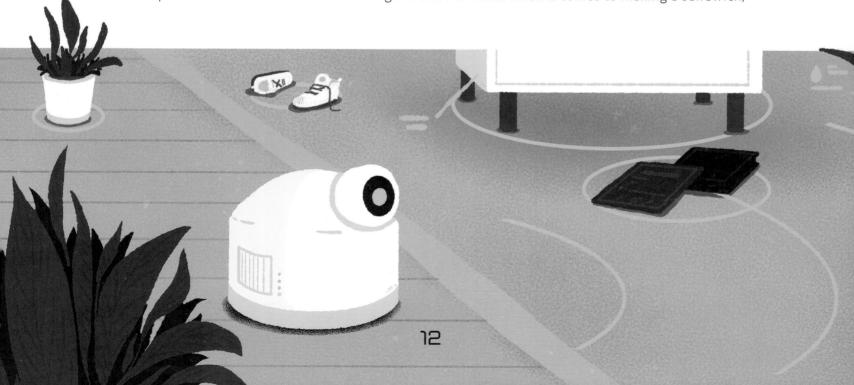

says Gennert. You know that jelly might be in the fridge, but clean plates and knives definitely won't be. This type of common-sense knowledge is something people acquire from living in the world every day. Robots don't have years of experience looking inside fridges and cupboards. But they do have one advantage over people: they can share one mind. "Once one robot figures something out, they could all know how to do it," says Gennert. So when one self-driving car detects and avoids a squirrel in the road, it can share that experience with every other car out there. They will all be better at dodging squirrels in the future.

Even with this rapid knowledge-sharing in full swing, you might have to train your personal robot on your kitchen and show it where to find what it needs. This type of training is another area where robotics has made exciting progress. In factories today, people no longer have to carefully program every movement of a robotic arm. Collaborative robots such as Sawyer have sensors that give them a basic understanding of their surroundings. To train Sawyer, a worker lifts and bends the arm, taking it through a task step by step. The robot remembers the motions and copies them. This would only work for your personal sandwich-making robot, though, if all the ingredients were in the exact same places all the time.

They do have one advantage over people: they can share one mind.

SURPRISE, SURPRISE

Of course, the same kitchen doesn't stay exactly the same day-to-day. This is the third big problem. The robot will face surprises! Someone might put the peanut butter in the wrong cupboard, or leave it out on the side, or even worse, finish it and put the empty jar back. Your little sister might grab the bread off the plate and start eating it while the robot is away getting the jelly. Your cat might fall asleep right in front of the cupboard door. The robot would need to safely handle these problems and obstacles. This would require constant real-time awareness of the world around it as well as the ability to predict possible future problems. For example, opening a door behind a sleeping cat might hurt the cat. Kitty would not be very understanding.

Computer scientist Matthias Scheutz and his colleagues at Tufts University are working on helping robots cope with potentially dangerous situations. Scheutz points out that people won't always give a robot safe instructions. A person could ask the robot to get the peanut butter without noticing that the cat is blocking the door. So a robot must be able to decide for itself if an action is safe. Scheutz' group has written software that allows any sort of robot to consider an action and decide whether it is safe or not. One robot they've worked with is called Nao. It's a doll-sized robot with a human-like body. In a demonstration, Nao stands on a small table. A member of Scheutz' team asks the robot to walk forward. If the robot obeys, it will fall to the floor. "But it is unsafe," says Nao. When the team member promises to catch the robot, it walks forward, off the edge, into the human's waiting hands.

The software Scheutz' team wrote for Nao is limited to a few specific types of situations. But they have an ambitious and extremely important goal: to make sure robots are safe.

SMART SYSTEMS

If you just want a robot to make you a sandwich, you can avoid all of these tricky problems. You can visit a cafe with a Bistrobot. First, you select the sandwich you want on a touch screen. Next,

bread slides along a conveyor belt under tubes that squirt out spreads like jam or peanut butter. Bistrobot doesn't have to pick anything up or find anything for itself. And its machinery is completely enclosed, which keeps things safe. But all it does is make sandwiches. It's more like a smart appliance than a robot.

"Ideas we see in the movies of robot assistants doing our chores are a bit far-fetched."

Smart appliances are much more likely in the near future than humanoid robot servants, say Rebecca Li and Elizabeth Hunter, PhD students in robotics at the University of Pennsylvania. "I think the ideas we see in the movies of robot assistants doing our chores are a bit far-fetched," says Hunter. "But I think that increasing levels of automation are very real." Automation means accomplishing a task without human oversight. For example, you might have a fridge that detects when things run out and orders more. That order could go to a warehouse filled with robots that find and pack items. Then a drone could bring fresh groceries to your house.

It may not ever make sense to build a single robot that can do any human job. Robots are more likely to continue to specialize. The more specialists there are, the more automatic life will become. You may have heard of the internet of things. This is an internet in which objects collect and share information. Specialized robots are just one part of this system. As the internet of things expands, homes, hospitals, farms, factories, and even entire cities are getting smarter. In the island nation of Singapore, a smart system alerts people about traffic jams or roadwork and also tells them where to find open parking spaces. In Barcelona, Spain, sensors buried underground tell gardeners when plants need watering. Eventually, smart systems and robots may run the entire world.

WHEN ROBOTS RUN SOCIETY

Living in smart homes and cities filled with robotic helpers sounds exciting, but to get there we'll have to overcome some serious issues. First of all, robots and smart systems make us more vulnerable to attack. Anyone with hacking skills can break into these systems. In 2016, hackers broke into a computer system and briefly shut down the electricity in Kiev, Ukraine. In the future, hackers could take control of self-driving cars, drones, or robot-run factories, farms, schools, or hospitals to cause destruction and mayhem. A robot that malfunctions on its own could also cause serious problems.

It takes a lot of energy to build and run robots and smart systems.

In addition, it takes a lot of energy to build and run robots and smart systems. A smart home filled with sensors and automated systems draws more power than a typical home. Developing and running robots takes a lot of energy, too. This energy still comes mostly from fossil fuels, which harm the environment. To fill the world with robots and smart systems, we must first find a cleaner source of energy (see Chapter 4). Money is another problem. These systems cost a lot to build and maintain. If only wealthy people and countries can afford the new technology, others will be left behind.

Speaking of money, if robots do all the work, how will people earn their livings? As self-driving vehicles replace human truckers and bus and taxi drivers, some will find new professions. But what if robots take all the jobs? People could end up homeless and hungry. To prevent this problem, some experts say that governments should pay everyone a universal basic income. But there's no guarantee that will happen, or that the money will cover all of a family's needs.

Even if the basic income idea works out, would you really enjoy a permanent vacation? Playing video games or hanging out with friends all day would be fun for a while. But eventually you'd likely start to get bored or even miserable. Human beings want to feel useful and successful. You might not always like school, but education, jobs, and careers provide a sense of purpose and accomplishment. Sports, games, art, music, and other hobbies could take the place of schoolwork and jobs, but only if people get the right materials and training to take part.

Would you really enjoy a permanent vacation?

Would you want a robot as your teacher or coach?

People may not want robots in certain jobs, even if the robot is perfectly competent. Would you want a robot as your teacher or coach? What about as a babysitter or nurse? Paro, a cuddly robot shaped like a seal, already helps comfort people in some nursing homes. Other robots help children with autism learn to communicate. Many of these robots make lifelike sounds and expressions. Some even recognize and mimic emotions. A humanoid robot named Pepper already helps people in hotels, banks, airports, malls, and other similar places. When someone seems joyful, Pepper smiles. If a person seems sad, Pepper says something comforting. But Pepper doesn't actually feel anything. People who use robots like Paro or Pepper may trust, befriend, or even love a machine that can't love them back. Is that morally wrong? Perhaps it doesn't matter as long as the person gets the care they need.

If robots aren't alive and don't feel anything, does that mean humans can treat them badly? Research has shown that a person who yells at a robot assistant is more likely to treat other humans with disrespect. If robots ever become human enough to build relationships with people, like C3PO and R2D2 in Star Wars, those robots may deserve basic human rights and freedom along with respect.

RULES FOR ROBOTS

The more we depend on robots, the more important it will be to make sure these machines are safe, secure, and follow human values when they make decisions. In a famous science fiction story by Isaac Asimov, robots must follow three rules: they may not harm humans, must obey humans, and must protect their own existence. Unfortunately, rules like these won't cover all situations. For example, if a child runs in front of a self-driving car, should the car swerve and crash, possibly killing its passengers? Or should it risk running over the child? The right thing to do depends on the specifics of the situation as well as a person's personal belief system.

Robots and smart systems are already here. Now, you and all the other people of the world have an important job to do. You will be the ones to figure out what robots' belief systems should be, and how robots can best help humans thrive, far into the future.

TELEPORTATION

Your alarm goes off in the middle of the night and you jump out of bed. Today is the day! You're going hiking... up Mount Kilimanjaro!

You quickly dress and grab some breakfast. Then you step into a machine the size of a fridge. You tap a screen to select your destination: Mount Kilimanjaro, the highest peak in Africa. Scanners pass up and down your body. You close your eyes and disappear.

But you haven't really disappeared. When you open your eyes, you're in a different machine. The door opens, and you step out into a vast expanse of bare rock peppered here and there with plants and small, scraggly bushes. A towering mountain peak rises above it all. You're looking at the summit of Kilimanjaro in Tanzania and it's already mid-morning here. You and your friends will spend a week hiking up, then teleport home from the summit. The machine behind you whirs, and out steps one of your friends. Soon, more friends have arrived, from all around the world.

Teleportation has made it possible to send anything from one place to another instantly. People no longer need cars, trucks, trains or airplanes to move things around. Everyone with a teleporter has instant access to food, medicine, and everything they need. No one gets homesick anymore because home is only as far away as the nearest teleportation booth. Parents work in distant cities or countries and still come home for lunch and dinner. No concert or football game is too far away to attend. School groups take day trips to foreign countries and on the weekends, families can visit any national park in the world, just to walk the dog. You can even zip over to the moon or Mars for a quick visit—teleportation is out of this world.

You can visit any national park in the world, just to walk the dog.

MATTER AND ENERGY

In the Harry Potter books, magical vanishing cabinets instantly transport people or things from place to place. And in Star Trek, a group of space explorers use a similar fictional technology called a transporter. "Beam me up!" they say, then they disappear from an alien planet and reappear on board their spaceship (or vice versa). Beaming is supposed to work like this:

Step 1: turn a person's body into a beam of particles and zap them to a new location

Step 2: put all the particles back together to form the person, exactly as they were before

Each of these steps comes with some huge, potentially unsolvable problems. In Step 1, the transporter has to break a person down into particles, small building blocks of matter. The smallest known particle is the quark. According to scientists' current understanding of physics, turning a person into a cloud of quarks requires a temperature of around 50 trillion degrees Fahrenheit. That's a million times hotter than the center of the Sun! No technology we know of can create such intense heat, and clearly the heat would kill you anyway. Dying in a sudden inferno (even if you get resurrected somewhere else) sounds quite unpleasant. It's unlikely very many people would volunteer to give a machine like this a whirl!

Dying in a sudden inferno sounds quite unpleasant.

But teleportation technology doesn't have to destroy and transmit the original body. If it can build a person from a beam of particles, then it should be able to use any particles. All the machine really needs to send is a blueprint, or instructions on how to put the person together. But how do you make a blueprint of a person? No one really knows. You'd at least need the person's genetic code plus an extremely precise brain scan. Researchers have calculated this comes to three hundred nonillion gigabytes of information. (A nonillion is a 1 with 30 zeroes after it!) "The number of neurons and the number of connections between them is beyond belief," says retired physicist Sidney Perkowitz. He is the author of *Hollywood Science* and taught physics for many years at Emory University. We regularly send and download movies and video games that are a few gigabytes in size, but even that takes some time. No existing technology could send or receive the information needed for a human blueprint in a reasonable amount of time.

And that's only Step 1! In Step 2, the machine has to follow the blueprint to essentially 3D print an entire living person out of particles. This does seem impossible. At the moment, researchers haven't yet figured out how to print a single living organ—see Chapter 6.

Plus, the person who steps out of the transporter is supposed to be the exact same person **You could suffer brain damage!** who stepped in. The uncertainty principle in physics means that you can't find out complete information about particles. So the blueprint of you won't be perfect. And 3D printers may make small mistakes, too. Those small mistakes could add up to big problems. On your way to Kilimanjaro, the teleporter might miss important information about your brain. Or the printer might mix up some neurons. You could suffer brain damage! Even if you arrive safely, what happened to the original you who stepped into the teleporter? Did that body die? Or did the teleporter create a duplicate you in the new location? Would you really want to either die or copy yourself every time you travel? Both options seem way too bizarre.

This is all so far-fetched that no serious scientist works on human teleportation. Perkowitz says that the ideas are fun to think about, but it seems impossible to implement them in any practical way. Teleportation will likely never get you anywhere faster than just climbing into a car, airplane, or rocket ship.

FROM VIRTUAL SPACE TO HOLOGRAMS

But guess what? You can already take a hike up Mount Kilimanjaro without traveling anywhere! You just have to put on a virtual reality (VR) headset. Virtual reality technology has existed for decades but the equipment has been bulky and expensive. Now, smaller, cheaper equipment can offer vivid experiences. Virtual reality doesn't move you to a new location. Instead, it brings the experience of being in a location to you. You see and hear things that aren't really there. The entire experience is a clever illusion that fools your brain.

For example, the Virtual Human Interaction Lab (VHIL) at Stanford University runs a simulation that makes you feel as though you are standing on a ledge over a deep pit. A narrow plank leads to another ledge. A third of the people who have tried the demonstration refuse to cross the pit even though they know they are really standing on solid ground. The perilous drop seems much too real.

Augmented reality (AR) technology brings avatars and virtual content into the real world. For example, you can already download an app that uses a smart phone's camera and speakers to create the illusion of a dinosaur tromping through your living room. Or, people can attend concerts and performances featuring virtual performers. Whitney Houston passed away in 2012, but an illusion of the famous singer went on tour in early 2020. Together, VR and AR are sometimes called XR, for Extended Reality.

The experience is a clever illusion that fools the brain.

XR technology can create an illusion of anyone—even you. If cameras capture your movements in three dimensions, then another device can project an avatar of you. Something called light field display technology creates extremely realistic three-dimensional projections of objects. These illusions are a lot like holograms from science fiction. Nima Zeighami, an XR developer, manages the online platform LeiaPix, which is like Instagram for light field display images. One user posted a purple flower.

Zeighami says, "It literally looks like a real flower you can reach out and pick."

During the coronavirus pandemic, people had to attend school, celebrate birthdays and holidays, and visit with family and friends through their devices. Some, tragically, had to say goodbye to loved ones this way. With XR, people can gather virtually in a way that feels much more real. Instead of seeing your friends or family or teacher on a screen, you can see them standing in your living room. It looks and sounds like they are really there.

ROBOT BODIES

Avatars and holograms can't interact with anything real, but robots can. People already use remote control robots to explore places that are dangerous for humans, such as the deep ocean or outer space. Rescue workers use robots or drones to survey a scene or search for survivors after a disaster. Some doctors use robots to visit patients. At the moment, using one of these robots feels like driving a remote-control toy while on a video call. But what if XR equipment could make it feel as if you're actually there?

You move your head and the robot's head moves the exact same way.

In the future, a person who wants to climb Kilimanjaro might rent a robot to take that hike. The robot would walk the trail. Meanwhile, the person at home would see through the robot's cameras, hear through its microphones, and feel through sensors on its body. They would feel as though they were on the mountain. XR developer Emre Tanirgan built a robot called DORA that offers a glimpse of this future. A person using the robot puts on a headset and hears and sees the world through the robot's microphones and cameras. At the same time, "the robot mimics head movement," explains Tanirgan. If you're using the robot and want to look around, you move your head and the robot's head moves the exact same way. Ideally, you and the robot would also have equipment that transmits touch, smell, or even taste. It should also let you walk, run, or climb wherever you want to go. Robotics technology and XR technology just aren't good enough yet to make this type of "teleportation" possible. But we'll get there, possibly within 20 years, says Tanirgan.

A NEW WORLD

In XR, we are no longer limited to words, sounds, and images to tell stories and share information. We can share whole-body experiences. "We don't just think with our minds," says Toshi Anders Hoo, director of the Emerging Media Lab at the Institute for the Future. "We think with our entire bodies, we think with our environment, we also think socially." In XR, instead of watching home videos, you can relive recorded home memories. Engineers can practice repairing holograms of jet engines before tinkering with the real thing. Surgeons can practice on virtual patients. Instead of learning through watching and listening, you can learn through going and doing.

People may spend too much time in XR.

But the realistic illusions of XR come with some tricky ethical issues. In order to work well, XR technology has to capture a ton of information about people, their behavior, and their surroundings. Whoever makes your XR equipment could potentially track where you are and how you move, talk, and act while using it. People will have to fight to protect this personal information.

Another potential problem is that people may spend too much time in XR. The internet, social media, and video games already draw people into imaginary worlds and distract them from the real world. Have you ever felt angry or frustrated when a family member or friend is too engrossed in

a device to notice you? If a person withdraws too much from their real-world friends, family, and responsibilities, a psychologist may diagnose an internet or gaming addiction. The experience of inhabiting a cool avatar or robot body could be even more addictive. In the story Ready Player One, a virtual world has become so vibrant and perfect that most people prefer the illusion. Taking on another body in another world is more than a distraction. You're completely cut off from reality.

Real-world experiences have a lot to offer

And real-world experiences have a lot to offer. For example, on a real hike up Kilimanjaro, you may see a rare serval cat and feel the joy of encountering another living being. You might get hurt or lost. You might push your body and mind to their limits, defy danger, and feel more alive as a result. A virtual world can only simulate discovery and risk. It's an illusion you can step out of at any time. So you likely won't feel the same exhilaration that you do on a real mountain. You also won't get as much real exercise or exposure to sunlight, which are both important for human health. Similarly, it's hard to imagine how a hug in XR could feel as comforting as one in reality. Even if you wore a vest to transmit the pressure of the hug, you'd still be hugging an illusion.

For all these reasons, XR is not meant to replace real world experiences. Rather, it offers a new way to have experiences that might not otherwise be possible. Anyone can hike Kilamanjaro in XR—even people with physical challenges. Also, the fact that danger seems real in XR but isn't can help people overcome fears or trauma. Anyone can hug in XR—even people who can't safely visit each other because of a pandemic. It's not the same, but maybe it's better than nothing.

Families can even hug loved ones who have died. This happened in 2020, when Jang Ji-sung and her young daughter Nayeon were reunited in VR. Nayeon had passed away in 2016 at the age of seven. The idea of interacting with illusions of lost loved ones may seem creepy or wrong. But is it really that different from looking at photos or videos of those you've lost? VR developer Liv Erickson says she has recorded experiences with her family using VR equipment, "so I can 'be with' my family in those moments as long as possible."

Families can even hug loved ones who have died.

"You can go anywhere, at any time, and at any scale."

Unfortunately, scammers could use virtual beings to fool people into trusting someone they shouldn't. Catfishing, when someone pretends to be someone else in order to steal money or trick someone, already happens online. This could become even more harmful when the fake person has a body, not just a profile picture. If VR illusions or XR holograms become convincing enough, people could be tricked into believing that someone or something fake is actually real.

But XR also has the potential to make the world a better place. The technology opens up new forms of connection and experience that aren't possible in reality. In one social VR experience, Hoo says, when many users play with the same object, glowing lines appear, connecting their chests. They all unlock new ways to use the object. It's like a visual group hug. When it comes to

"Who you are born as doesn't matter as much as thoughts, feelings, and ideas."

traveling, you can do more than teleport. "You can go anywhere, at any time, and at any scale, and you can go there with anyone," says Hoo. You can fly like a superhero over a city, shrink to ride through the air on a tumbling snowflake, or observe the moment of the Big Bang.

You can also become whoever you want. You can literally walk a mile in someone else's shoes. "Who you're born as doesn't matter as much as thoughts, feelings, and ideas," says Zeighami. You can use this freedom to explore different perspectives. For example, the VHIL created a VR experience of life as a homeless person. In one scene, other people try to take your things as you ride a bus to stay warm. The experience builds empathy and compassion. Experiences of life as part of a different culture, race, ethnicity or gender could have a similar effect. We could use XR to teleport into other places and other ways of being to better understand each other and our world.

CITIES IN SPACE

A sleek ship rises into the sky, then bursts through Earth's atmosphere and into the blackness of space. You gaze out the window at the blue, green, and white sphere that is planet Earth, then settle in for a journey that will last for several months.

Finally, you approach your destination. It's a red world wreathed in clouds. "We will shortly be arriving on Mars," your captain says. "Please fasten your seat belts for landing." The spaceship descends and lands with a bump. You exit through a tunnel and enter a vast dome filled with growing plants. Machinery and computers hum as they work to maintain the dome's air quality and temperature. A staircase leads down into a vast system of tunnels and caverns. There's an entire city beneath the Martian soil.

"We will shortly be arriving on Mars," your captain says.

Similar cities exist throughout the Solar System. A base on the moon oversees asteroid mining. Thousands of people live on large, free-floating space stations. Meanwhile, a few groups of brave explorers have set off for other solar systems. They will live their lives on board spaceships, never touching solid ground again. Someday, their children's children will land on an alien world. Humanity has spread far beyond Earth. Today you're on Mars, but the entire galaxy is there to explore.

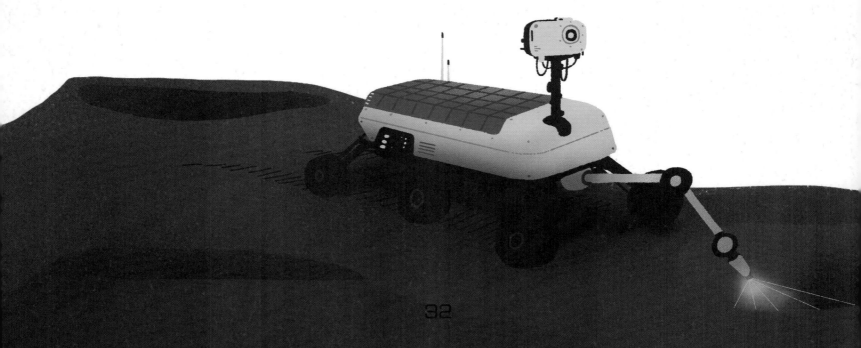

ROCKET SCIENCE

Astronauts have already walked on the moon and lived on board the International Space Station (ISS). Scientists have landed robotic vehicles, called rovers, on Mars and sent probes to planets, moons, asteroids, and comets. So why don't we already have a base on Mars? In 1969, the US president considered a mission that would have landed humans on Mars in 1982. But the US instead chose to build the Space Shuttle. It ferried people and supplies back and forth from space for 30 years. The fact is, we already have the technology to explore space, and we've had it for a long time.

High costs have prevented most mission ideas from getting off the ground. Sending stuff into space is very expensive (and dangerous to boot). Earth's gravity and thick atmosphere push back against anything trying to escape. To overcome Earth's hold, a craft must move very, very fast. It has to achieve escape velocity—which is around 7 miles per second. At that speed, you could get from New York City to London in

Most of the propellant on a rocket is there to push the rest of the propellant into space.

eight minutes. Also, rockets burn propellant in huge explosions to get going fast enough. Since there are no petrol stations in space, a rocket has to carry all the propellant it needs on board. That makes the rocket very heavy. The heavier the rocket, the more propellant it needs. Most of the propellant on a rocket actually pushes the rest of the propellant into space!

As a result, there isn't a lot of room left on board for what's called the payload. The payload is the astronauts or equipment going into space. In 2012, sending a pound of payload, or about one football, into space on the Space Shuttle cost around

$10,000. Imagine how much the luggage for your trip to Mars would cost! Thankfully, private companies are finding cheaper ways to build and launch rockets. In 2020, the company SpaceX successfully launched two astronauts using the rocket Falcon 9. Over the previous few years, they had shown that they could safely recover and reuse this rocket. In the past, each space launch had required lots of other new equipment. Being able to reuse rockets makes a launch less expensive. It only costs around $2,500 to send a pound to space on Falcon 9. And the company hopes to cut that cost in half. That might be cheap enough to make a trip to Mars affordable. Elon Musk, the founder of SpaceX, plans to land humans on Mars by 2026. "We have the technology to actually get everybody there," says Kennda Lynch, an astrobiologist at The Lunar and Planetary Institute in Houston, TX. "It's getting people on the ground and making sure they can survive that we're still working on."

A COLD RED DESERT

What would it be like to try to survive on Mars? Imagine living in Antarctica, then take away the air and most of the water and make things even colder. (Oh, and take away the penguins, too. You don't get any of those on Mars.) The lack of air is the biggest problem. Earth is covered by a thick blanket

Imagine living in Antarctica, then take away the air and most of the water and make things even colder.

of gases (mostly nitrogen and oxygen) called the atmosphere. Mars has a thin atmosphere made almost entirely of a gas called carbon dioxide. People would suffocate if they tried to breath it. They need oxygen to survive.

We have solved the air problem before, on board the International Space Station. The ISS turns water into air using electrolysis. This process uses electricity to get oxygen for the astronauts to breathe out of H2O (water) molecules. The water on the ISS originally comes from Earth, but it would cost too much to ship water to Mars. If Mars has any liquid water, it lies buried under an ice sheet nearly a mile thick. Martian soil contains tiny bits of ice. But it will take a lot of energy to get the ice out of the soil and melt it. This energy could come from solar panels or possibly a nuclear reactor. So, a Mars settlement needs energy to extract water to make air. And it needs an enclosed space or a habitat to contain that air. Of course, the settlement will also need water for drinking, washing, and farming so it will make sense to recycle the water. On the ISS, all of the wastewater—even pee—is cleaned and put right back into the water system. The astronauts on the ISS have a running joke, "Yesterday's coffee is tomorrow's coffee."

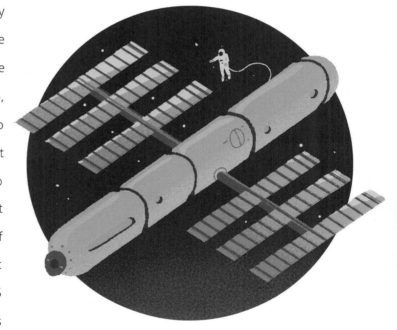

The ISS gets a lot of help from Earth. Regular resupply missions bring food, medicine, and equipment. The astronauts on board can chat with Earth at any time. A Mars settlement wouldn't have this kind of support because Mars is much too far away. The two planets orbit around the sun at different rates. They're only close enough together for trips back and forth every two years. Even then, the trip would take around six to eight months with our current technology. This vast distance slows

On the ISS, pee is cleaned and put right back into the water system.

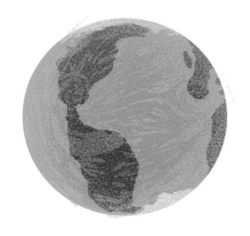

down messages, too. If you text your friends on Earth during a visit to Mars, it would take between three and twenty minutes for the message to arrive. So, a Mars settlement would have to generate energy, extract water, make air, grow food, make most of its own supplies, and solve all of its own problems.

Even setting these things aside, a major problem remains for people living on Mars. It's probably something you wouldn't guess. Mars has no magnetic field. Why does that matter? The Sun, stars, and other cosmic objects spew out lots of energy, called radiation. We see some of it as visible light, but there are also many invisible types of radiation. Some types damage living cells, making cancer more likely. Luckily, Earth's magnetic field deflects most harmful radiation away from our planet. We can wear sunscreen to protect ourselves from the radiation that does make it through. On a spacecraft or on the surface of the Moon or Mars, no field means no shield. All of the astronauts who have been to the moon or the ISS have been exposed to high levels of radiation, but only for short periods of time. People traveling to Mars would be exposed for the entire months-long journey. And anyone who lived on Mars would need something much thicker than sunscreen to protect themselves. They'd need thick walls or caves. Robert Zubrin is an aerospace engineer and president of the Mars Society. He predicts that people on Mars, "will live most of their lives in underground colonies."

If you text your friends during a visit to Mars, it would take between three and twenty minutes for the message to arrive.

HOME SWEET MARS

Making Mars a place where people can live won't be easy. And even if we could build the perfect Mars habitat here on Earth—with systems that generate energy, harvest water, make air, grow food, block radiation, and more—we still have to get it to Mars. Remember, rockets can only carry a certain amount of payload. The lighter and more compact, the better. Structures that inflate or unfold could work, but lightweight plastic probably wouldn't last long in the harsh environment of Mars.

Another fascinating idea is to grow structures on Mars out of fungus.

A better idea might be to build something on Mars. Engineer Berok Khoshnevis of the University of Southern California came up with a way to turn the soil on Mars into buildings. This soil has a lot of sulfur in it, and sulfur melts easily, explains Khoshnevis. "When it cools down, it sticks to a lot of things." He designed a robotic system that uses the sticky sulfur to form concrete-style bricks or 3D print entire structures out of Martian dirt. Another fascinating idea is to grow structures on Mars out of fungus. Mushrooms and other fungi make strong, root-like threads that grow just about anywhere. "These threads have been tested to be stronger than concrete and lighter than bricks," says Jason Derleth. He's an executive at NASA Innovative Advanced Concepts (NIAC), the organization that funded the research. Builders could set up a plastic scaffold and add bits of fungus. The carbon dioxide in the Martian air would help the fungus to grow and it would only need a little water and food. Bacteria, algae or even human waste could feed it. Once fungus covers the entire scaffold, it could die but those strong threads would remain.

No matter how we build a habitat on Mars, human settlers would be stuck within it, unable to venture out without space suits, and completely dependent on their life support systems. It would be like a prison. To most people, that doesn't sound like a pleasant way to live. For a settlement on

Mars to become a permanent home, something has to change—either the planet, or the people. Changing conditions on a planet to make it more Earth-like is called terraforming. On Mars, the first step would be warming up the planet. This could be done with giant mirrors in space that aim sunlight at the surface. Alternatively you could set off nuclear bombs, as Elon Musk has somewhat jokingly suggested.

> Changing conditions on a planet to make it more Earth-like is called terraforming.

> As Elon Musk has put it, Mars is "a fixer-upper of a planet."

As the planet warms and ice melts, the gases trapped inside would be released, and the atmosphere would thicken. This is similar to the climate change happening here on Earth. Except on Mars, a thicker atmosphere and warmer planet would be a good thing for humans. These ideas are still the stuff of science fiction. In 2018, NASA scientists calculated that terraforming Mars would be impossible with today's technology. Future technology could make terraforming possible, but even then, the process is likely to take around a thousand years or more. As Musk has put it, Mars is "a fixer-upper of a planet."

The other option is to change people. That means genetically engineering humans or modifying human bodies with robotics to make it possible to live more comfortably in a place like Mars. We'll explore how this might work in Chapter 8.

FLOATING CITIES

People like planets. We're used to living on solid ground. But is Mars really the best spot for a settlement? Maybe not. Derleth points out that a settlement on a space station would be easier

loating City
ove Venus
ht actually
he easiest
e to have a
colony."

settlement like this could orbit Earth and Mars in an endless figure-eight loop. To get resources, a space station might rely on asteroid mining. Asteroids contain materials that people could use to make water, propellant, building materials, radiation shields, and more.

Weightlessness would be a problem for people living on a space station. It may seem fun to somersault in the air, but long-term weightlessness isn't good for human bodies. Muscles and bones quickly lose strength and extra fluid behind the eyes causes vision problems. In the 1970s, the physicist Gerard O'Neill came up with detailed plans for a self-sustaining habitat inside a giant, free-floating cylinder. The ship's rotation would simulate gravity. The habitat would get its energy from the sun and would grow its own food. Other researchers have proposed donut-shaped or spherical habitats. But no one is currently building such a structure.

What about our other neighbor, Venus? Well, the planet isn't very welcoming. The pressure at the surface would crush a submarine, and the temperature, at around 869 degrees Fahrenheit, is hotter than an oven turned up to max. Sulfuric acid, a chemical that eats through human skin, forms clouds in the lower atmosphere. But the upper atmosphere is different. Here, the temperature, pressure, and gravity are all comfortable for humans. "It's actually the most Earth-like environment outside of Earth in the entire Solar System," says Derleth. "Although there are numerous challenges, a floating city above Venus might actually be the easiest place to have a colony in the entire Solar System outside of the Earth."

Planets with even more Earth-like conditions may exist in other star systems—but we don't know of any technology that could reach them. The journey to Alpha Centauri, the closest star system, would take around 80,000 years using rockets. A nuclear engine might get the trip down to 1,000 years. That's still a long time. And so far engineers have only experimented with this technology. A tiny computer chip attached to something called a light sail might be able to get there in as little as

BEYOND EARTH

Many experts point out that humanity cannot survive far into the future if we stay on Earth.

We've talked about how people might live in space or on other planets. But should they? Space travel is perilous. When things go wrong, even minor things, everyone on board a spacecraft or living in a space settlement may die. This is a risk that some are willing to take, but for different reasons. And those reasons are important. Many experts point out that humanity cannot survive far into the future if we stay on Earth. "Our future cannot be limited to just this one planet," says Khoshnevis. If some catastrophe were to wipe out life on Earth, other worlds could carry on our civilization. For example, a settlement on Mars likely wouldn't get infected by a pandemic on Earth. "I think it's important that we strive to have a self-sustaining city on Mars as soon as possible," Musk says. He sees it as life insurance for all of humanity.

A future in space is not only about avoiding disaster. Zubrin says that more homes for humanity would mean more opportunities for innovation. People could learn new ways of living. "What if when we go to Mars, we don't have trash?" asks Danielle Wood, head of the MIT Media Lab's Space Enabled research group. Resources would be so scarce on Mars that the people living there would have to find creative ways to reuse their waste. For example, plastic waste could fuel 3D printers. These innovations could then help solve the trash problem here on Earth.

As we expand our civilization into space, we must make sure that we avoid repeating humanity's past mistakes. Some world leaders pursue space as a way to increase power and prestige. Some companies hope to mine moons or asteroids. The explorers who colonized many parts of Earth during the 15th to 19th centuries had similar goals. Sadly, they killed or harmed native people and ecosystems to reach those goals. As far as we know, nothing lives on the moon or Mars. But does that make it OK for one person or group to decide to build a base or start terraforming? All of humanity should have a say in how we explore space. For example, some cultures see the moon as a sacred place that shouldn't be altered. Their voices matter. So do the voices of scientists who want to study other planets, explorers who want adventure, and artists who want to preserve the beauty of other worlds. Your voice matters, too. So think carefully about how you want our future in space to look.

Also, keep in mind that many problems humanity faces won't be solved by moving to another planet. In the near future, it is more important to solve our problems here on Earth. For example, if we invent the technology to terraform Mars, we should first use it to fix Earth's climate problems. "Earth is home. It's our best home base," says Lucianne Walkowicz, an astronomer at the Adler Planetarium in Chicago. We know Earth is a great place to live. If we can't look after it, how can we expect to transform an alien world into a new home that will last?

"Earth is home. It's our best home base."

No matter where we live, we will need to figure out how to care for our environment and our fellow humans with kindness and respect. Walkowicz points out that our future in space is not just about what kind of habitat we'll build, or what type of spaceship we'll need. They ask, "How do we want to live together? How can we live in ways that allow everyone to thrive?" These types of questions matter. We will need to answer them whether we stay on Earth or journey out into the distant reaches of our galaxy and beyond.

ENDLESS FUSION ENERGY

You arrive home from school and turn on some music. Electricity flows into the speakers. It travels from a power plant that houses something very special: a trapped star.

It shines in the same way as our sun or other stars in the night sky but fits into a single room. Engineers figured out how to tap into the energy of the stars and create very small ones here on Earth. Now, all the cities of the world have their own trapped stars. They provide enough electricity to power all of human society, now and far into the future.

Thanks to this plentiful source of energy, fossil fuels have become a distant memory. People no longer burn oil, gas, and coal to make electricity. Cars and other vehicles don't rely on gas, either. They've switched to electric engines. Homes and businesses use electric heat. The trapped stars do not pollute or spew harmful gases into the environment, either. So the world's climate has become stable. You don't have to worry about climate change leading to higher sea levels, rampant forest fires, flash flooding, or droughts and famines. Smog no longer descends on the world's busiest cities. These trapped stars make cheap, clean, safe, practically endless energy. But how? The secret is fusion energy.

WHY THE SUN SHINES

Fusion happens when two atoms smash together and merge into a larger atom. This process releases lots of energy. But atoms don't like to fuse. The closer they get to each other, the more they push away. It takes extremely high temperatures and pressures to force them together. Inside the sun and other stars, where it is really hot and dense, the conditions are ideal for fusion. Here, atoms merge

to create the elements that make up our universe. The energy from these nuclear reactions is what makes the stars shine. The sun and all stars are giant fusion power plants.

Current nuclear power plants on Earth use fission, a nuclear reaction that splits atoms apart. Both fission and fusion reactions release a huge amount of energy from a very small amount of fuel. More importantly, these reactions do not release any of the gases that worsen climate change.

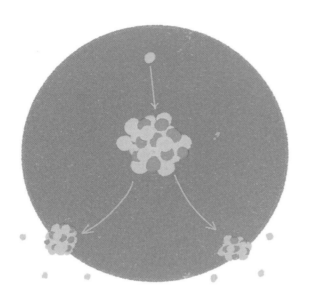
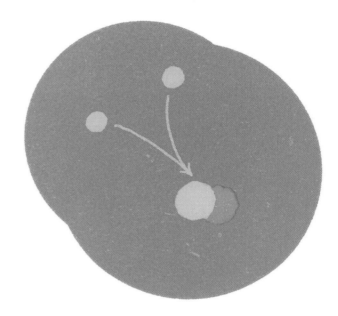

Fusion does not produce dangerous waste.

Unfortunately, the waste from a fission plant is dangerously radioactive. Accidents or disasters may release the dangerous stuff into the environment. Fusion is safe and doesn't produce dangerous waste. The fuel to power a fusion reaction can be made from sea water. As Saskia Mordijck, a fusion scientist at the College of William & Mary in Virginia, puts it, "Who wouldn't want to live in a fusion-powered world?"

TAMING STARS

Sadly, we don't yet have fusion power plants. But we already know how to make a star here on Earth. Scientists fused atoms in the lab for the first time in 1932. And in 2020, twelve-year-old Jackson

Oswalt became the youngest person to achieve fusion. He built a machine called a fusor. It looks as cool as it sounds—inside a small glass chamber, a purple orb glows and sparks as atoms fuse.

We already know how to make a star here on earth.

It's totally awesome that people can make stars. But it takes a ton of energy to get them to shine. All the fusors and fusion reactors that have been built so far suck up more energy than they produce so they are useless as power plants. We do know how to make one fusion device that generates a lot more energy than it takes in. It's the most devastating weapon humans can build—the hydrogen bomb. When the bomb goes off, a fission explosion triggers fusion. This produces a massive amount of energy. But a hydrogen bomb also destroys everything for up to ten miles in every direction and poisons the environment with harmful radiation. This is clearly not the answer.

So, the big challenge facing fusion scientists today is not how to build stars, but how to tame them. We have to work out how to keep our trapped stars shining in a way that makes useful, safe energy.

HOT AND DENSE

To get atoms to fuse, you have to force them together and crank up the heat. The hotter and closer together the atoms are, and the more time they spend like this, the more fusion reactions you get. If you can make enough fusion reactions happen, then the energy from the reactions will trigger more and more fusion. This process is called ignition and it's essential to get more energy out of fusion than you put in. It's similar to lighting a campfire. After you provide a spark, the fire keeps itself burning as long as you keep adding fuel.

So, what is the fuel? It's hydrogen, the lightest, simplest and most abundant element in the universe. Engineers can easily produce fusion fuel from hydrogen found in seawater. Once you've got the fuel, you have to heat it up. The fusion reaction most engineers hope to achieve has to reach around 270 million degrees Fahrenheit to keep itself going. That's ten times hotter than the center of the sun. Yikes! At this temperature, the fuel becomes plasma. Plasma is a state of matter beyond solid, liquid, and gas. Hot plasma desperately wants to spread out, but its atoms must crash together to fuse. So you have to keep them trapped inside something. But what? Such a hot mass will vaporize glass, metal, or any other container. Despite these difficulties, scientists have come up with several imaginative techniques to tame stars.

Such a hot mass will vaporize glass or metal.

FROM INVISIBLE FORCEFIELDS TO GIANT LASERS

Many fusion researchers use an approach called magnetic confinement. They use powerful magnets to control and contain the plasma. Plasma is made of charged particles, and a magnet forms invisible fields around itself which change how these particles move. This means that if you can twist magnetic fields into just the right shape, you can trick plasma into swirling around and around instead of flying apart. The magnetic fields form an invisible forcefield or cage. A donut-shaped magnetic cage is called a tokamak. Another device that looks like a twisted donut is called a stellarator. Neither cage is perfect. The hotter the plasma gets, the more it tries to escape. Escaping bits of plasma mean fewer fusion reactions. A typical experiment lasts just seconds to minutes, and no one has yet managed to get the combination of heat, density, and time high enough to reach ignition. But this will happen soon, experts say. "I know we can do it," says Mordijck.

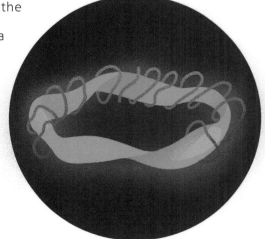

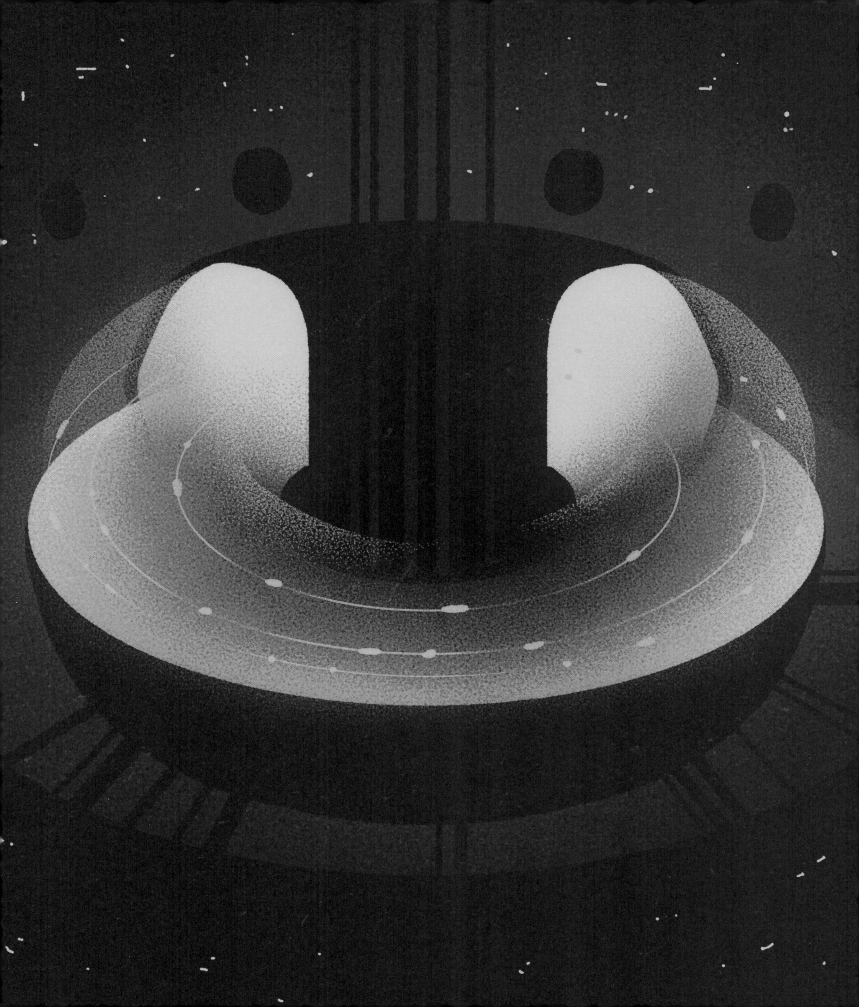

Tammy Ma, a physicist at Lawrence Livermore National Laboratory in California, works on a different approach called laser fusion. She gets to fire the largest laser in the world, which is at the National Ignition Facility, a building so huge it could fit three football fields inside. During a fusion experiment at the facility, 192 laser beams fire from all different directions onto a tiny pellet around the size of a grain of rice. The pellet contains fusion fuel. The laser explodes the outer layer of the pellet, forcing the middle to implode. Every time we fire the lasers at the NIF, says Ma, "we are the hottest place in the solar

"We really are making stars."

system. We really are making stars." Ideally, the imploding fuel gets hot and dense enough to reach ignition. This hasn't happened yet, but teams around the world are inching closer. Within ten years, Ma believes, they'll get everything just right and will achieve ignition. She says, "it will be a huge celebration. I think it will be a little like landing on the moon."

A massive new tokamak in France named ITER may guide the way to a future with fusion energy. Thirty-five countries are working together to build the colossal machine. Simulations say it should generate ten times as much energy as it consumes. Meanwhile, other teams around the world are working on smaller machines. Some combine elements of laser fusion and magnetic fusion.

SOLVING CLIMATE CHANGE

Glaciers are melting and sea levels are rising, too.

Fusion scientists and engineers will almost certainly find a way to produce energy, but they still need to spend time and money testing many different ideas. Fusion scientists in the US plan to build a working fusion power plant by the 2040s.

Fusion is coming soon, but unfortunately not soon enough. Climate change is already happening. Glaciers are melting and sea levels are rising, too. Natural disasters such as fires and hurricanes have become more common and more damaging than in the past. The United Nations Intergovernmental Panel on Climate Change (IPCC) has urged the world to make rapid and far-reaching changes. Young activists including Greta Thunberg are raising awareness of the crisis we have on our hands. Perhaps you have participated in a climate strike at your school.

Climate change is happening because carbon dioxide (CO_2) and other greenhouse gases in air trap sunlight, warming the planet. The amounts of all these greenhouse gases are increasing because every machine that burns coal, oil, or natural gas spews them out. The most straightforward way

CLIMATE FRIDAY
STOP GLOBAL WARMING
CLIMATE STRIKE
SAVE OUR PLANET
STRIKE
ACT NOW
YOUTH FOR CLIMATE
SAVE OUR PLANET
CLIMATE STRIKE

We have to find alternate energy sources now.

to slow down climate change is to stop using fossil fuels. We can't just stop using our machines and technology, though, so we must switch to other energy sources. By 2050, the IPCC says, we need to get to zero emissions. That means we need to absorb and trap as much CO_2 as we release. We can't wait five or ten or twenty years to start working toward this goal. We have to find alternate energy sources now. "It's a race against time," says Arturo Dominguez of the Princeton Plasma Physics Laboratory in New Jersey.

We already have lots of options. We can replace gas-powered engines with electric ones that run on batteries. We can get electricity from the sun with solar panels or from the wind with turbines. We can harness the motion of fast-moving water with hydropower dams or heat from deep in the Earth with geothermal plants.

Nuclear fission power plants can produce electricity anywhere.

Making electricity from the sun, wind, water, or Earth releases almost no harmful gases. However there are drawbacks. For example, solar panels and batteries are made of rare metals that pollute the environment and may run out. Also there's no sunshine at night and the wind doesn't blow all the time, but people use electricity all the time. We need better batteries to store electricity from these sources and smarter grids that can handle different sources of electricity. Similarly, not all places have easy access to fast-moving water or geothermal energy, but people need electricity everywhere.

Nuclear fission power plants can produce electricity anywhere, at any time. We already talked about some of the dangers of this energy source. Thankfully, engineers are building new nuclear fission power plants that are much safer than those in the past. These new plants can reuse waste as fuel and can shut down safely in a disaster.

ENERGY FOR ALL

Switching the world to new energy sources won't be easy. People and their governments will have to spend money on new vehicles, new heating systems, new power plants, smarter electrical grids, and more. These changes are expensive and time consuming. And no replacement energy source offers the perfect solution. Fusion seems perfect, but may very well come with drawbacks that we don't yet know about.

We have to make sure that the entire world has energy.

We also have to make sure that the entire world has access to energy. Right now, the richest countries of the world use the most energy. These are the countries that have caused climate change and continue to make it worse. They also have the resources to withstand worsening weather and other disasters. Developing countries and poor communities did not cause climate change. In many of these communities, families can't light their homes at night or use TVs, cell phones, or computers. Now, they face the devastating impacts of climate change without enough resources to help.

While new energy technology is still being developed, poor communities will likely need fossil fuels to survive and thrive. Wealthy people and countries should take responsibility and change their energy habits first. They should also "help poor countries deal with the mess they have inherited," says Rose Mutiso, co-founder of the Mawazo Institute in Nairobi, Kenya and research director of the Energy for Growth Hub.

The entire world will have to come together and work towards change.

Mutiso is optimistic that new technology can solve the world's energy problems. The ideal energy technology could even be something that no one has imagined yet. She says, "we need a lot of miracles, but human history is full of many examples of our ingenuity in the face of difficult challenges."

Simply inventing a new energy technology won't change the future, though. The entire world will have to come together and work towards change, she says. Presidents, lawmakers, community leaders, CEOs, and even regular people must cooperate. Only then will we be able to reach a future in which every family has all the energy they need, as well as a healthy and safe planet to call home.

FOOD FOR ALL

You're hungry. So you wander into the kitchen. A refrigerator-sized maker machine greets you with a glowing display. You tap to select a hamburger.

The machine hums and whirs as it works. After a short wait, a plate appears. Then a steaming hot burger and a fresh-baked roll pop out. You tap to add ketchup and a pickle. When you're done eating, you tap an icon showing a glass of juice. Zip, sizzle, and out pops a cup. Freshly squeezed orange juice fills it up.

But there are no hamburgers or oranges inside the machine. It takes in air, water, soil, sand, garbage, and other cheap, easy-to-find raw materials. Then it breaks all this stuff apart into atoms and molecules. Next, it follows a blueprint to rearrange these into any kind of food, drink, material, or object.

It breaks stuff apart into atoms and molecules.

The machines have spread to every corner of the planet.

A maker machine can even make robots, computers, or the parts needed to build a copy of itself. The machines have spread to every corner of the planet. They have transformed the world. Factories, farms, supermarkets, and shopping centers no longer exist because no one needs them. The roads and skies and seas are quieter because no one has to order or deliver stuff any more. The raw materials the machines take in are free and available everywhere, so everyone with a machine has instant, easy access to food, clothing, tools, medicine, robots, computers, and any other items they could ever need or want.

MOVING ATOMS

Could a maker machine ever exist? The one we just imagined moves atoms and molecules into any arrangement. An entire scientific field, nanotechnology, investigates how to manipulate the world at these very small scales. Researchers can detect or even move single atoms around using an instrument called a scanning tunneling microscope. It earned its inventors a Nobel Prize in 1986. The only thing is, the microscope is huge and can only move one atom at a time. It takes at least a trillion atoms to make a lump of stuff the size of a grain of salt. This process is way too slow and tedious to work on large objects.

Could a horde of very tiny machines—smaller than the eye can see—move atoms and molecules into any arrangement? Some famous physicists have pondered this idea. But no one knows how to make even one such machine. The world works differently at very small scales. Forces that affect big things, like gravity, no longer matter much. Forces that attract things together matter more. In the nano-scale world, water seems thick as honey, says Simone Schuerle. Nano-sized things can be as sticky as honey, too. If a nano-sized machine let go of a tool, it wouldn't drop. It would remain stuck. So you can't take a large robot that moves stuff around and shrink it down in size. You have to build a bot suited for the unusual, nano-scale world. Schuerle develops nanotechnology for medical purposes at ETH Zurich. She has built nanomachines that do amazing things, including carrying medicines directly to tumors. But the idea

Every living thing was once a single cell.

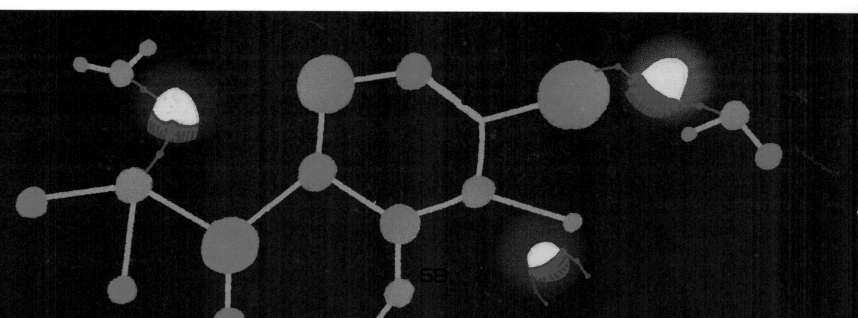

that nanomachines could ever construct an entire meal out of atoms "seems a futuristic fantasy," says Schuerle.

Cells, bacteria, fungi, and other very tiny living things are already at home in the nano-world. They move around and regularly build chains of molecules that they use for attack, defense, and growth. Every living thing was once a single cell, even a blue whale or a giant oak tree. It may never be possible to make a machine or a swarm of tiny robots that can build an entire object out of individual atoms. However using microbes or cells to build things is an entirely different story. Researchers in the field of synthetic biology have already engineered microbes and grown batches of cells in order to produce medicines, fuels, chemicals, and many other things people need.

"If you want a table, then you should just grow a table."

For example, researchers found a way to grow only the fluffy part of a cotton plant, which is the main ingredient for many fabrics. Other researchers have grown algae that feed on sunlight and carbon dioxide while producing gases that can be used as fuel. Cells or microbes are usually grown inside stainless-steel vats called bioreactors. As long as the vat provides a comfortable environment with plenty of food, then the tiny community inside will act like a living factory, churning out useful stuff. The possibilities are endless. "If you want a table, then you should just grow a table," says Luis Fernando Velásquez-García, an engineer at MIT who is working on a way to grow wood in a bioreactor. Instead of chopping down trees, cutting them up into boards, and then fixing those boards together, he says, you could some day coax plant cells to grow into any shape you want.

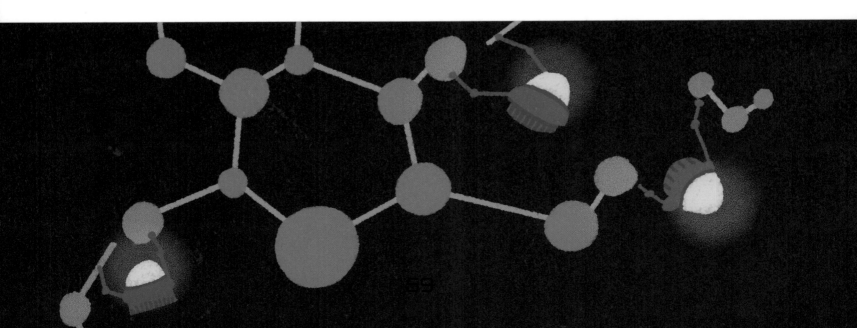

PLANTS IN DISGUISE

Synthetic biology is also helping us reimagine how we produce meat. You can walk into most supermarkets right now and buy a package of Impossible Burgers. The patties are made entirely out of plants but taste a lot like real meat. How is that possible? All food is a combination of water, protein, fat, and carbohydrate. If you understand exactly what meat is made of, you can find those same ingredients in plants. Then you can duplicate meat's texture, taste, smell, and even how it changes color as it cooks.

The main ingredient in meat is protein. The Impossible Burger uses powdered protein taken from soy and potatoes. Food scientists then send the powder through an extruder, which is a tube that heats, squeezes and steams the protein, giving it a more meat-like texture. Next, it is cut up and dried. "What you have at the end looks a lot like breadcrumbs or stuffing," explains M.J. Kinney. She is a food scientist and the founder of FareScience, a company that develops plant-based meat products. Meat also contains fat. In plants, fat is called oil. The Impossible Burger uses coconut and sunflower oils.

So far, so good. But these plant proteins and oils don't taste like real meat. The flavor of animal meat comes mainly from a molecule found in blood. That molecule is hemoglobin, an iron-rich protein that carries oxygen and gives blood its red color. One specific part of a hemoglobin molecule, called heme, contains most of the iron and most of the meaty flavor. Soy roots also contain heme, though not very much of it. So researchers took the soy genes that make heme and put them into yeast DNA. (This is called genetic engineering. We'll learn all about it in Chapter 7.) This yeast grows happily in bioreactors, producing plenty of heme. Food scientists mix together the dried-out plant protein, oil, and heme with water, spices, and an ingredient called a binder to make sure it all sticks. They form it into a patty and the burger is ready to cook and eat. Other companies have found formulas that work to mimic other meats. You can find plant-based chicken nuggets, sausage, and even tuna fish.

A MAGIC WAND

With the help of synthetic biology, we can turn plants into something that tastes a lot like real meat. We could grow tables or even entire homes from plant cells, or use microbes to make fuels and medicines. These technologies are cool, but growing is not the same as making. The futuristic maker machine from the beginning of this chapter is more like a magic wand from a fairy tale. Wish for a gown and glass slippers, and *poof!* You're ready for the ball.

Huge 3D printers with robotic arms have crafted bridges, houses and buildings.

A 3D printer is a bit like that magic wand. In the future, if you need glass slippers (or regular shoes), you probably won't have to go to a store or wait for an online order to arrive. You could just scan your feet, choose your own colors and patterns, and print out a new pair. They'll fit you perfectly. Today's 3D printers can't create something out of nothing, though. They only reshape materials into new forms.

The most common type squirts melted plastic through a nozzle onto a surface, layer by layer, gradually building an object from bottom to top. As the plastic cools, it hardens. Food printers squeeze out cookie dough, chocolate, or frosting into stunning shapes. Other 3D printers use lasers to stick metal dust together or to form a solid object inside a tank of liquid. Huge 3D printers with robotic arms have crafted bridges, houses, and buildings out of concrete-like materials.

In the near future, having a 3D printer could be as common as having a microwave oven. People might use them to print everyday things such as toothbrushes, headphones, or clothing. Or maybe they'll buy cartridges of flour, sugar, proteins, oils, and so on, and use those to print out meals.

In the far future, we may even have shape-shifting materials. Engineers may create tiny chunks of matter, also called voxels, that could change shape as needed, sort of like Lego bricks. You could wake up in your bed, then ask your bed to become a chair and table. You might put on a t-shirt that thickens into a sweater when you go outside. You may even carry around a small blob that can become a spoon, a hammer, scissors, or any other tool you might need.

PRINTED MEAT AND BUG BURGERS

People of the future will also print new body parts. Bioprinters already turn living cells into pieces of skin and other tissue (See Chapter 6). If that's possible, so is printed meat. To get enough cells for a hamburger printer, a future meat factory would likely grow them in bioreactors. In 2013, researchers at Maastricht University in the Netherlands served the world's first cell-based hamburger to a group of food critics, including Hanni Ruetzler. "It's close to meat, but it's not that juicy," she said. The main problem with this first burger, though, was that it cost around $325,000 to make! Costs have come down quite a lot since then, but expense is still a major problem.

Why do we need to change the way we eat meat? Raising farm animals for meat takes way more land and water than growing the same amount of fruits and vegetables. Farm animals have the second largest impact on climate change after fossil fuels. Plus farmers give them a lot of antibiotics to help them grow and, as a result, some disease-causing microbes have learned to resist these drugs. Finally, it would be nice not to kill living creatures in order to eat. Forming meat from plants or growing meat in bioreactors could help solve these problems. But meat-growing factories will still consume electricity and make pollution. A better idea may be chowing down on bug burgers. Crickets, mealworms, ants, and other creepy-crawlies are packed with protein and nutrients. Many cultures around the world already consume insects and farmers know how to grow lots of them with

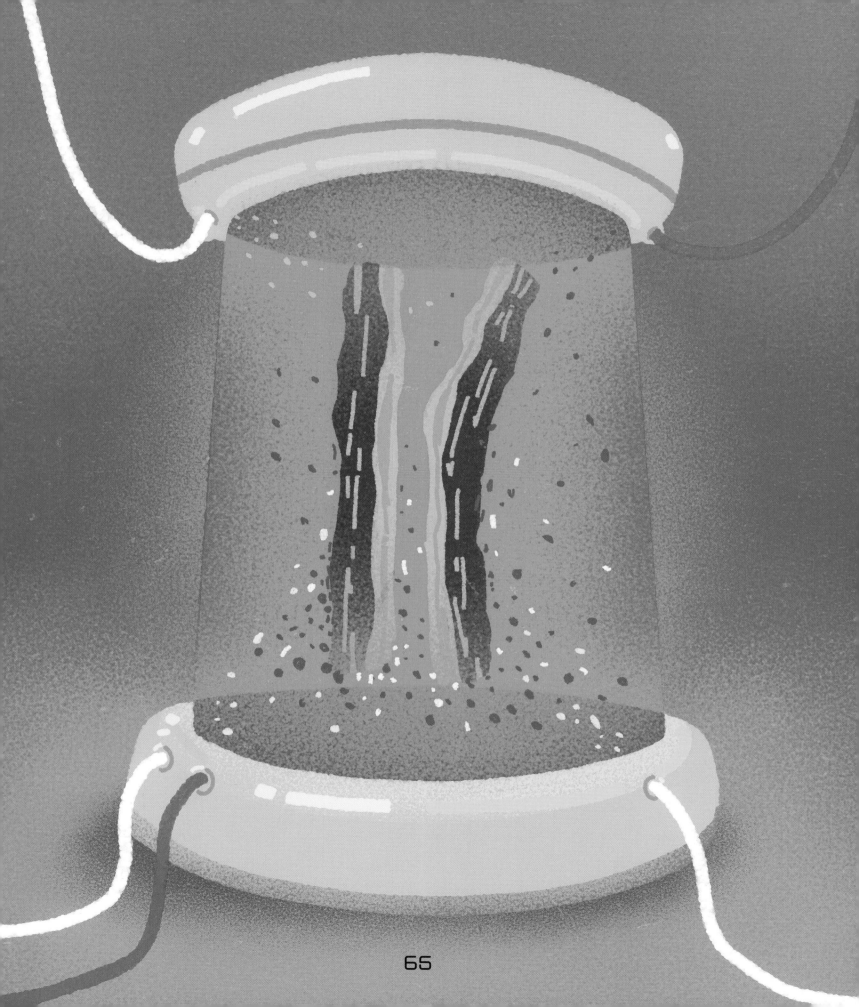

very little land and resources. People who don't already eat bugs may have to get over the "gross" factor and get used to the idea.

THE POWER TO MAKE ANYTHING

A machine that can make almost anything sounds amazing. Unfortunately, not everything people make will be useful or safe. People have already figured out how to make guns on 3D printers. What if someone prints plates and cups out of a toxic plastic meant only for robot parts? They could get very sick. What if a teenager designs and prints a skateboard that breaks or a robot that catches fire? 3D printers make it easy to bring bad ideas—as well as good ones—to life.

On the positive side, 3D printing could help solve some big problems. Right now, a vast network of planes, trains, ships, and trucks carry materials, parts, and products around the world. All those vehicles pump out greenhouse gases and pollution. 3D printers could produce things only when and where they are needed. That's great, but factory assembly lines use much less electricity per item than a 3D printer. And the plastics most 3D printers use aren't easily recyclable. If home 3D printers get cheap and popular, we might start printing out loads of items that we don't really need. A new way to make plastic garbage is the last thing the world needs right now. Plastic waste chokes the world's landfills and oceans. Tiny bits of plastic have worked their way into our food system and our bodies, harming our health in ways that we don't yet fully understand.

We have to be careful that our remaking respects the planet.

For 3D printing to actually help solve environmental problems, we must develop machines that use less energy. And we must feed them with recyclable or reusable materials. "We need to find ways to print in waste product, food byproducts, recycled glass, sand, even dirt," says Mark Ganter, a mechanical engineer at the University of Washington in Seattle. Future technology will allow us to remake the world around us in astounding ways. We just have to be careful that our remaking respects the planet. Hopefully, it will also help clean up the mess we've already made.

LIVING FOREVER

You blow out the candles on your birthday cake.
Your family and friends clap and cheer. "Happy 300th birthday!"
someone shouts.

Then everyone gathers around as you pass out slices. Many of the people gobbling up cake are just as old as you or even older. But all of you look 20 or 30. A few days after the party, you have an appointment with your doctor. Like all adults, you get regular injections of a serum made specially for you. This therapy acts as a kind of fountain of youth. It prevents aging by giving your body the tools it needs to repair and rebuild itself endlessly. You may have been around for 300 years, but each individual cell in your body is much, much younger.

The serum keeps you youthful and vibrant but it can't fix everything. What if you have an accident and damage a part of your body beyond repair? No problem! Every hospital has a lab that grows replacement organs and limbs. When a part of you breaks, you get a new part. Only the most severe accidents and very rare illnesses cause death. There's a cure for almost all human ailments. You could live forever.

When a part of you breaks, you get a new part.

SPARE PARTS

Could you really reach the age of 300 or beyond? "Advancements in science make this potentially a real possibility," says Dr. Daniel Weiss. He's a doctor at the University of Vermont. No one in recorded history has lived past 122 but the average human lifespan has been creeping steadily upwards, from around 30 in the 1800s to 72 today. In many countries, it's not nearly as unusual as it once was for a person to celebrate their 100th birthday.

To keep people alive much longer than that, doctors have to repair or replace worn out body parts. This is called regenerative medicine. Has anyone you know received a new hip or knee joint made from metal or plastic? These body parts are fairly straightforward to repair or replace. Mechanical systems can take the place of some organs as well. For example, people with heart problems may be fitted with mechanical valves, or even an entire mechanical heart if they need one. A man named Barney Clark received the first total artificial heart transplant in 1982. When he woke up from the surgery, he told his wife, "Even though I have no heart, I still love you!"

At the moment, we don't have mechanical replacements for most major organs. Instead, surgeons today use healthy organs from living donors or from people who have recently died to replace diseased or damaged ones in their patients. Unfortunately, the number of people who need new organs far surpasses the number of spare parts available.

Scientists hope to change this. Researchers are investigating ways to form or grow brand new body parts. But how? Most take one of these intriguing approaches: 3D-printing organs; filling old, dead organs with new, living cells; or modifying animals so people can use their organs.

CAN PIGS SAVE OUR BACON?

Researchers aim to grow human organs inside host animals. A pig's organs happen to be roughly the same size as a human's. Also, these animals reproduce quickly and have large litters. Could we harvest their organs and put them into humans? No. The human body treats any animal organ as a foreign invader and destroys it. But scientists are finding ways to disguise animal organs so they seem less threatening to a new body. In a 2018 study, two baboons lived for six months with pig's hearts in their bodies. Other researchers aim to grow human organs inside host animals. The result is called a chimera—a creature that contains parts from more than one species. Researchers have injected human cells into pig embryos and let them develop for several weeks. So far, no human-pig chimeras have been born.

You're definitely not alone if you think it seems creepy to breed pigs with human organs in their bodies. While lots of people think it's OK to kill animals for food or medical purposes, it's illegal to kill people. So how do you draw the line between a human and a part-human animal? Another problem is that in Judaism and Islam, two of the biggest religions in the world, it is forbidden to eat or touch pork. The leaders of these religions are already debating whether or not using a body part from a pig to save a person's life might be allowed. Even if you don't follow one of these religions, you may feel that it is wrong to kill animals for any reason, even if it means saving a person's life. Many people hope for a better, more humane way for everybody to be able to receive new body parts.

You may feel that it is wrong to kill animals for any reason.

COLOR BY NUMBERS

Thankfully, there are alternatives. Someday, scientists may be able to grow or print entire organs from a patient's own cells. Weiss' lab works on growing human lungs outside of a body. They start out with a real human or pig lung, which doesn't even have to be healthy or working properly. Next, the researchers wash away all the old cells. This is called decellularization. (Try to say that five times fast!) The process gets rid of everything except the scaffolding that cells grow on. At this point, the lung looks ghostly white but is the same size and shape as before. The next step is the hard part. A lung contains over 40 different types of cells. Some make up the muscles and others form airways and blood vessels. Like filling in an especially difficult color-by-number, researchers have to get each cell type to grow and fill in only its parts of the scaffolding. It's a tough task. For now, Weiss' team works on small, thumb-sized pieces of lung tissue. They've seen these pieces begin to behave like real lungs. But Weiss predicts it will take at least another five years before an entire lab-grown lung is ready for transplant.

Researchers can already 3D-print pieces of human skin or bone.

Other researchers hope to use 3D printing or other manufacturing tools to form human organs and other body parts from scratch. Researchers can already 3D-print pieces of human skin or bone. They can also make hollow body parts. Dr. Anthony Atala, a surgeon at Wake Forest Institute for Regenerative Medicine, has been transplanting engineered bladders and windpipes into patients for 20 years. He uses his patients' own cells to grow the new parts. One of his patients, Luke Massella, received a new bladder as a child in 2001 and is still doing well.

Crafting skin or a bladder is one thing. An entire working lung, heart, liver, kidney, or pancreas is another story. Adam Feinberg is a bioengineer at Carnegie Mellon University. He says, "We're still very far from making an organ," but he believes we will get there.

One of the biggest problems with printing whole organs is keeping all the cells in the tissue alive. Living tissue contains a web of blood vessels and other channels, many of them much thinner than a strand of hair. Like tiny roads, these channels bring cells the stuff they need to survive. They also carry cells' waste away.

Some researchers are trying to recreate this intricate channel system. Jordan Miller, a bioengineer at Rice University, has printed something that mimics a single air sac from a human lung complete with blood vessels and an airway. The only thing is, it's ten times bigger than an actual air sac and took 5 hours to print. A human lung has around 600 million of these air sacs. In 2021, NASA ran a contest that challenged teams to create chunks of organ tissue at least 1cm (about 0.4 inches) thick that can survive for 30 days. The winning team received $300,000. Engineers still have to find ways to print organ tissue more quickly and more cheaply. For now, it's still very important for people to sign up to be organ donors, says Miller.

No matter how doctors get a replacement organ, they still need to put it into a patient's body. That means cutting the person open. Also, there's one organ that you wouldn't want to replace: your brain. It contains your memories, everything you have learned, and in some ways, everything it is to be you. It may be possible to someday copy your memories and personality from one brain to another—but would you still feel like you after such a procedure? No one knows. Also, as we learned in Chapter 2, gathering and transferring complete information about an entire brain is almost impossibly difficult and unlikely to happen any time soon.

There's one organ you wouldn't want to replace: your brain.

THE FOUNTAIN OF YOUTH

What if doctors didn't have to transplant new parts? What if the body could repair its tissues and organs or even grow new ones all by itself, like a lizard re-growing a lost tail? In fact, your body already contains a small population of very special cells, called stem cells, that act like little factories. They pump out replacements for cells that wear out. But they can't handle major damage.

Adding extra stem cells could be a little like sending in rescue crews to assist with clean up after a hurricane. The local workers may get overwhelmed by a big disaster, but with extra help, they could rebuild more easily. Extra stem cells might be able to repair a weakening heart or even increase the number of healthy brain cells and prevent dementia. Someday, scientists hope, stem cell therapy could cure heart disease, Alzheimer's, cancer, baldness, and any number of other diseases. "Doctors and scientists are working hard to make it safe and possible one day," says Dr. Saranya Wyles, a physician at the Mayo Clinic. Other researchers are working on nanotechnology and engineered microbes that could someday swim around inside people and make repairs. However, these treatments aren't ready yet.

Many people desperately need cures for diseases now. Sadly, some scammers take advantage of this desperation and offer cures that do not actually work. Many supposed stem cell treatments are not backed by any research and could cause harm. Similarly, the internet is chock full of "miracle" cures for aging and a multitude of other conditions. Be very wary of any product or treatment that seems too good to be true—it probably is.

Replacing or repairing body parts might keep a person alive for several hundred years. But would it really be possible for a person to look and feel young for that long? Scientists will almost certainly find ways to slow aging or reduce its damage. But it seems unlikely that they will ever figure out how to completely prevent old age. Robin Holliday, a geneticist and expert on aging, wrote that "aging cannot be reversed." His reasoning was that there are too many things that go wrong over time. We'd never be able to fix all of them, all at once.

Scientists will almost certainly find ways to slow aging or reduce its damage.

Many of the processes that lead to aging are things the body simply has to do. One of them is eating. Turning food into energy also releases molecules that damage cells. But even if doctors managed to find a way to stop this type of damage from happening, they'd still have to stop many other aging processes, all without shutting down any of the systems that keep the body functioning.

THE PERILS OF IMMORTALITY

We should also ask ourselves whether living forever is really a good idea? If living to 300 or older means dealing with an aged, fragile body for decades or longer, would you still want that for yourself or your family? Some people might reconsider the idea of living forever if to do so they'd have to give up their independence, mobility, mental sharpness, memories, or more.

Others might be more willing to make these sacrifices in order to stick around as long as possible. Dying is scary, so living a very long time—even in an old body—may seem ideal. But death also forms a clear end point that completes the natural cycle of every living thing. Death and aging are important themes in many of our most beloved stories and works of art. The contrast between living and dying, being and nothingness, can make life feel even more precious and something to treasure while it lasts. For people who believe in a soul that moves on to an afterlife, death is a transition and an essential part of religious faith. Would life still feel as meaningful if you knew you wouldn't ever die?

On a more practical level, an immortal or ancient population would not be good for the world. If everyone had babies and then went on to live for centuries, the population would quickly grow out of control. What would all those people eat? Where would they live? If all these long-lived people aged but never died, caring for all of them could get ridiculously expensive or even impossible. "There comes a time in each person's life where we have enjoyed our living, and now it is time for us to let others continue to live," says Lawrence Prograis, a retired bioethicist from Georgetown University.

Would life be meaningful if you knew you wouldn't die?

Some thinkers have imagined immortal humans spreading out into outer space to make room for themselves. Others have wondered if an immortal population might stop having children. Right now, raising kids is the most important and fulfilling part of many people's lives. Would we really choose to live in a world without them?

Population growth is just the most obvious problem to contend with. As older generations die and new ones come of age, society is often reborn with new social norms and ways of thinking and acting. Would culture ever evolve or change if its politicians, artists, scientists, scholars, CEOs, and other leaders lasted forever? Would extremely ancient people continue to create, invent, and discover new things? Living forever could become monotonous, repetitive, and boring.

We also have no idea how extremely long life might impact the mind and the self. Would immortal people be happy or would the endlessness of life seem daunting and lead to mental health conditions? Could our relationships with friends and family last for hundreds or thousands of years, or would we drive each other bonkers? No one knows the answers. But medicine may take us to a future where we find out.

PET DINOSAURS

//

"Rex! Here boy!" you call. A dinosaur romps over. It's a small one, just a few feet long from head to tail. It tilts its feathered head and stares at you with beady, bird-like eyes.

You toss a treat into the air, and Rex leaps for it, shrieking with a call that sounds like a cross between an eagle and a wolf. After the two of you play for a while, you put Rex in his pen and head out to the zoo to see a new enclosure that just opened. A train takes you past several different kinds of living dinosaurs. You see Apatosaurus, Stegosaurus, and even Tyrannosaurus rex. Your train passes a woolly mammoth and a saber-toothed cat. Other zoos have Plesiosaurs and Pterosaurs. All of these animals were once extinct, but scientists have brought them back to life.

Finally, you reach the new exhibit. In the middle of a field of green grass, a majestic creature drinks from a stream. A unicorn. It has the body of a white horse, but a single, curved horn grows from its forehead. In another habitat on the other side of the tracks, a giant, lizard-like creature swoops out of the air and lands on a branch, folding a pair of leathery wings. It's a dragon. You gaze wide-eyed. This is even more amazing than you'd imagined. Fantasy has become reality.

THE RECIPE FOR A LIVING CREATURE

In the Jurassic World movies, scientists create living dinosaurs. How? They find dinosaur blood inside ancient, preserved mosquitoes. The blood contains DNA. Coiled-up chains of DNA molecules sit inside almost every living cell. Like a recipe, DNA contains instructions that tell a body how to grow and maintain itself. The movie scientists use the recipe they find to grow baby dinosaurs. In real life, this won't work. Scientists have never found any dinosaur DNA, not even in preserved mosquitoes. (They've looked.)

After an animal or plant dies, its body, including its DNA, breaks down. Some frozen, mummified, or preserved bodies do hold onto traces of DNA for thousands or even hundreds of thousands of years. But the last dinosaurs went extinct over 65 million years ago. Is it even possible for DNA to survive that long? "No," says Beth Shapiro, a molecular biologist at the University of California, Santa Cruz. She should know. Her team found and sequenced one of the oldest genomes ever, from the bone of a horse that died around 700,000 years ago. The bone had stayed frozen that entire time. Even then, she says, "the DNA was in terrible condition." Instead of long strands, "It was really tiny, broken-up pieces of DNA," she says.

Could we still have a real life jurassic Park?

Even if zero traces of dinosaur DNA remain, could we still have a real life Jurassic Park? "Yes," says Jack Horner, a dinosaur scientist at Chapman University in Orange, California. Scientists probably won't be able to bring back the same dinosaurs that went extinct. But they should be able to create animals that look a lot like them. They should also be able to create new animals that never existed, including ones that resemble mythological dragons or unicorns. "We know we can do it," Horner says. "It's just a matter of finding the recipe."

The complete recipe, or genetic sequence, for a living thing is called its genome. If you were to print the entire human genome, it would fill up 800 dictionaries. Segments of DNA, called genes, are like the steps in the recipe. They control appearance and the way a body functions. A living thing gets its genes from its parents, typically half from its mother and half from its father. Your unique set of genes determines your hair and eye color, your height, whether you can roll your tongue, and many other things about you—but not everything! Your lifestyle and the experiences you have in your life also make you who you are.

Mutating or changing a gene will alter the recipe. This can change how the body works—before or after birth. DNA mutations happen occasionally in all living cells. Sometimes, a mutation has no effect. Other times, it leads to cancer or another disease. And sometimes, it gives the living thing an advantage. Over time, as parents pass genetic changes on to their children, living things evolve into new species. People have also found ways to make genetic changes happen on purpose. One method has been around since ancient times: breeding. Farmers have developed many new kinds of plants and animals this way.

Here's how it works. Let's say farmers want a larger horse. They will choose horses that are already a bit bigger than normal and mate them together. When the foals grow up, the farmers will again choose the biggest ones to mate. Over time, this will lead to bigger horses. The same process can lead to drastic changes

Breeding can lead to drastic changes in any species.

in any species. Dog breeders managed to create huge Great Danes as well as tiny Chihuahuas. A wild banana is short and stubby with large, hard seeds inside, while farmed bananas are long and seedless. Wild corn was once the size of a peanut with ten or fewer hard, bland kernels. Sweetcorn cobs have become a thousand times bigger—and much sweeter and juicier, too. Almost every food you eat was bred to be bigger, bolder, juicier, sweeter, easier to grow, easier to eat, easier to harvest, or easier to store and transport than it once was. Creating new living things through breeding takes decades or even centuries. But using technology to alter DNA works more quickly and can even introduce traits that don't already exist in a species.

A NEW TOOL FOR GENETIC ENGINEERING

Genetic engineering includes any tool or technique that alters DNA. This controversial technology can introduce totally new ingredients and steps into a genetic recipe. And it skips the long trial-and-error process of breeding. But first, scientists must figure out which genes control a trait, such as size. Often, several genes control one trait. Also, one gene may influence several different traits. To solve this puzzle, scientists must spend serious time and effort testing out changes on cells in the lab.

Scientists must figure out which genes control a trait.

In the 1970s, researchers figured out how to introduce genes from one species into another. This creates a genetically modified organism (GMO). For example, a specific jellyfish gene makes any living cell glow green under a certain type of light. Scientists have used the gene to make glowing rabbits, pigs, monkeys, and cats. (This wasn't just for fun. The glow is an easy way to detect whether a genetic change has actually happened.) Plant scientists have used genes from other species to engineer new crops. For example, they've made corn that fights off insects and rice with added nutrients.

Then, in 2012, Jennifer Doudna and Emmanuelle Charpentier pioneered the use of a groundbreaking new technology called CRISPR. They won the 2020 Nobel Prize in Chemistry for their work. CRISPR seeks, finds, and slices out sections of DNA. Other tools can then paste in new DNA if needed. CRISPR is cheap and easy to use. Scientists can use it to make GMOs. Or they can remove or repair genes that already exist in a genome. This is called gene editing. For example, in 2016, researchers found a gene that makes cut up mushrooms go bad. They used CRISPR to remove it, creating mushrooms that stay fresh longer. In 2020, scientists used gene editing to create vaccines very quickly during the COVID-19 pandemic, saving many lives.

MAMMOTH PARK

Scientists are also using CRISPR and other tools to piece together recipes for animals that have gone extinct. Several teams of researchers are working on the woolly mammoth genome. Some preserved mammoth bodies still contain DNA, because the last of these huge creatures went extinct just over 5,000 years ago. Even then, finding enough to put together a complete genome isn't easy. It's as if the recipe has gone through a shredder, and all scientists have to work with are a handful of tiny pieces. They have to try to put together the entire recipe from these scraps. Even if they can cobble something together, the damaged DNA won't work inside a living cell. They need complete DNA from a living cell to create a living animal.

The Asian elephant is the mammoth's closest living relative. So some scientists aim to edit elephant DNA to make an animal that has woolly mammoth traits. George Church of Harvard University has identified the genes that gave the mammoth its woolly coat, large ears, extra fat, and more. In 2015, he made copies of some of these genes and used CRISPR to stitch them into the DNA of living elephant cells. The cells survived in dishes in a laboratory. Eventually, scientists may be able to make these same edits in a female elephant's egg cell. But growing that egg into a baby is a whole new problem. The technology to do this doesn't exist yet. An elephant probably can't carry and give birth to a mammoth. Still, scientists may eventually make an elephant with some mammoth-like traits.

Scientists need complete DNA to create a living animal.

CHICKEN-O-SAURUS

What about dinosaurs? They also have living relatives—birds. Believe it or not, the humble chicken is Tyrannosaurus rex's distant cousin. Even without any shreds of ancient DNA to work from, scientists have managed to identify some of the genes that separate birds from their dinosaur ancestors. For example, they have found some genes that prevent birds from developing dinosaur-like claws or teeth in the beak. Deleting these genes could erase several hundreds of thousands of years of evolution. Other traits, like tail length, are more complex. Horner's team is studying how to control tail growth. They pick a gene, then "turn it on or turn it off and see what happens," says Horner. No mutant dino-chickens hatch during any of these experiments. The team does the genetic changes inside chicken eggs. Then, they let the embryo grow for a few days before discarding it. They want to understand the dinosaur recipe thoroughly before bringing a new baby animal into the world.

If scientists can grow a dinosaur tail on a bird or mammoth hair on an elephant, just imagine what else they could do to alter life on Earth. If a trait can exist in nature, then genetic engineers can probably create it. Making a fire-breathing dragon isn't very likely since no real creatures breathe fire. But making a winged lizard should be possible. And a horned horse should be even easier. Scientists have already shown that they can remove horns from cattle. In 2015, two hornless calves, Spotigy and Buri, were born. Scientists at the company Recombinetics had edited the calves' DNA to prevent horns from growing. Real, living creatures that look like unicorns, dragons, mammoths, dinosaurs, or whatever else you care to imagine could really exist someday thanks to genetic engineering.

Making a winged lizard should be possible.

PLAYING GOD

Just because scientists can do something doesn't mean they should. Some people feel that it is morally wrong to interfere with developing embryos or attempt to create new lifeforms using genetic engineering. Some have referred to the practice as playing God—perhaps humans aren't prepared for this type of power.

Using genetic engineering to create new plants or animals comes with risks. A genetic change may cause disease, suffering, or other unwanted results. Researchers experiment extensively on cells in the lab before creating any living animals or plants. But even then, many living animals or plants may have to die or suffer before a genetic change is perfected. So scientists and citizens must carefully consider whether the benefits of developing a new lifeform outweigh the risks.

A genetic change may cause disease or suffering.

Editing cows so that horns never grow seems more reasonable when you learn that cow horns pose a danger to humans and other cows. However, editing crops to make them resist weed killers allowed farmers to use more weed killers, a practice which is bad for the health of the soil and the ecosystem. An anti-GMO movement has spread throughout the world, leading to bans or product labeling in many countries. The real problem, though, is not the technology of genetic engineering. It is how some companies have used it to support harmful farming practices. Activists also worry that the companies creating genetically modified seeds are controlling what farmers plant.

The good news is that GMOs and genetically edited foods are perfectly safe to eat. And some scientists are working to engineer crops that could help feed the world in the future. Samuel Acheampong, a PhD student at the University of Cape Coast in Ghana, is engineering a sweet potato with added nutrition. He hopes that someday, people will "eat less, but get all they need." In addition, engineered crops could produce more food using less land and water. Genetic engineering could also help endangered animals and plants survive. Climate change threatens to wipe out many types of coral. Researchers in Australia hope to use genetic engineering to help coral survive the extreme changes happening to their ocean home.

A PLACE IN THE WORLD

Cattle, sweet potatoes, and coral already have a place in the world. Extinct and mythological animals do not. What will happen to them once they are born? The mammoth was a very social animal. Mothers cared for their young for three years. The first baby mammoth wouldn't have any adults to keep it company or show it what to eat or how to behave. A baby dinosaur would be in the same situation. These animals' natural habitats no longer exist. What impact might they have on creatures that exist now? Ecosystems and food chains in nature are very delicate. A new animal could harm existing species. We could create places for new animals to live in zoos or parks, but what if they escape, just like in the Jurassic World movies?

Ecosystems and food chains in nature are very delicate.

Molly Hardesty-Moore is a graduate student in ecology at the University of California, Santa Barbara. When she thinks about the idea of a real Jurassic World, she says, "I start to feel nervous." Ecologists study how all the living things in an environment interact. Hardesty-Moore argues that it doesn't make any sense to bring an animal to life unless we have good reason to believe that it will thrive and help to heal existing ecosystems. For example, a small insect-eating bat that lived on Christmas Island in the Indian Ocean went extinct in 2009. Bringing it back could prevent the ecosystem from becoming overrun with insects.

Mammoths could have a positive impact as well. When they stomped across Siberia, they spread seeds and nutrients in their dung, unknowingly planting lush grassland. When they went extinct, the ecosystem suffered. Bringing these giants back could restore plant and animal life to a cold, remote part of the world. One man is preparing for their return. Sergey Zimov started Pleistocene Park in 1989. Over the past decades, he has reintroduced plants and animals that still survive in other parts of the world. Any future mammoths (or mammoth-like elephants) could live here. "The hope is that someday we will have large herds of them, if that's what society wants," says George Church.

What does society want? Some say we can't justify spending time and money to bring back animals that are already gone—we should help the ones that are still here to make sure we don't lose them forever. However, many species have gone extinct because of the damage that humans have done to their habitats. You could argue that we have a responsibility to bring these species back and help them thrive.

We should help the animals that are still here to make sure we don't lose them.

The idea of creating dinosaurs, unicorns, or dragons is harder to defend. Hardesty-Moore says, "If you're just putting horns or wings on an animal because it's cool, that doesn't seem to be a justifiable reason." It doesn't seem fair to bring new animals into the world just for our entertainment, especially once we can play with whatever magical creatures we want in virtual reality. New living creatures may suffer during experiments to perfect the recipe. Also, caring for these animals may be tough. "Every cool kind of dinosaur is bigger than your house. It's not going to fit in the garage," Horner points out. It's probably not going to be very comfortable in a zoo or park, either.

There is no clear right or wrong answer to the question of whether we should create new animals, plants, or other living things. Every case is unique and comes with its own risks and benefits. But what is clear is that CRISPR and related tools have given humanity incredible power to alter life as we know it. It's up to us to use this power for good. If we are responsible with the technology and respectful of other lifeforms, we could transform and repair our world in marvelous ways that could benefit plants, animals, and humans.

SUPERPOWERS

You're shooting hoops with some friends. But
this is no old-fashioned basketball court.
You're on a huge football field with a hoop set up
in one end zone. And the hoop is as tall as a house.

From the far end of the field, you eye the rim and shoot the ball. Swish! Running to get the ball

feels just as effortless as making the basket. You sprint with what was once the speed of an Olympic

athlete. When you get to the hoop, you leap over it in one jump, the typical celebration for a

successful shot. Special clothing gives you an extra boost.

Your friends clap and cheer, but you know that what you did was not all that

exciting or impressive. Everyone you know has super strength, speed, and agility.

Everyone has super senses, too—eyes as sharp as an eagle's and ears that hear

Everyone you
know has super
strength, speed,
and agility.

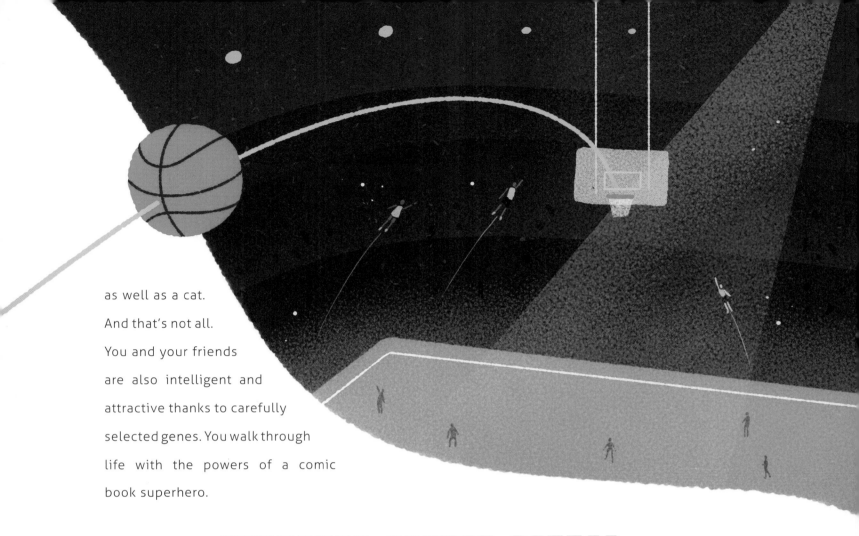

as well as a cat.
And that's not all.
You and your friends
are also intelligent and
attractive thanks to carefully
selected genes. You walk through
life with the powers of a comic
book superhero.

STRONGER, FASTER, BETTER

Could you ever really become Black Panther, Iron Man, Wonder Woman, or Superman? No person today can leap over tall buildings (or basketball hoops) in a single bound. But advances in technology and medicine may take us to a future in which superpowers that seem amazing, or even impossible, become a normal part of life. One route to superpowers is mechanical. Like Iron Man's robotic suit, special clothing or robotic body parts may someday bestow super strength, speed, or other powers.

Many sports stars today already get an extra boost from special equipment. For example, shoes with extremely springy soles help runners go faster. In 2019, Eliud Kipchoge ran a marathon in less than two hours which was an astonishing feat and a world-first. The special shoes he wore may have helped push him along just a little faster than he otherwise could have gone. Back in 2008 and 2009, full-body 'super suits' helped swimmers break more than 100 world records.

Other technology replaces or alters part of the body. Already, some people without certain body parts or body parts that no longer work may use robotic arms, legs, feet, or hands. Mechanical parts can help with vision and hearing as well. A cochlear implant delivers sound directly to the brain. These mechanical body parts are incredible technology, but usually can't do everything that a biological body part can. As robotics technology improves, though, mechanical body parts could give people extraordinary abilities.

In science fiction, a person or animal with both biological and mechanical body parts is sometimes called a cyborg. In the future, cyborgs could create new types of music and art. Imagine playing the piano or the guitar with extra fingers. Imagine seeing colors invisible to human eyes or hearing sounds that human ears can't usually pick up. Cyborgs could also experience new types of adventure. People already put on special footwear to climb, ski, skate, and hike. But if you're replacing an entire leg or foot or hand, you can entirely redesign the way that limb works.

Hugh Herr, an engineer at MIT, was one of the pioneers of cyborg limbs. Herr lost both of his legs below the knee in a climbing accident as a teenager. Just a few months after the accident, he began tinkering with his prosthetic legs. He realized that there was no need for them to look like human legs so he designed new versions that were perfect for climbing. He shrank the feet, so he could balance on tiny footholds more easily. He added blades to the toes to grip rock crevices. He lengthened the legs to reach distant toeholds. And he made the legs extremely lightweight, which meant he could carry the weight of his body more easily than someone with bulky human legs. "I returned to my sport stronger and better," said Herr.

Curving blades often propel runners and jumpers who are missing one or both legs or feet. In 2018, the German athlete Markus Rehm pushed off with a blade leg and jumped an extraordinary 27.8 feet: far enough to clear the length of a pickup truck. The mighty leap set a record for para-athletes and would have beat the gold-medal-winning distance jumped by American Jeff Henderson, who has two human legs, in the 2016 summer Olympics. A few runners using blade legs have come close to matching records set by runners using human legs. Do blade legs allow a para-athlete to jump farther or run faster than someone without blade legs? They might. For this reason, Rehm hasn't been allowed to compete in the Olympics. But a para-athlete still has to work incredibly hard. Blade legs don't turn a person into a superhero.

Insects have tough outer shells called exoskeletons. Engineers use that same name for robotic suits that fit over the body like clothing. Someday, you may be able to hop into an exoskeleton and move with greater speed, lift with greater strength, or perform other superhuman feats. Hugh Herr said, "Fifty years from now when you want to go to see your friend across town, you're not going to go in a big metal box with four wheels. You'll just strap on some wild exoskeleton structure and you'll run there."

This might sound fun, but today's exoskeletons don't look nearly as cool as Iron Man. They look more like harnesses with backpacks attached. Brendan Quinlivan, a researcher at Harvard University, helped design an exosuit that gives a boost to a person as they walk or run. Today's suits are each designed for a specific activity. The same suit can't help a person run and also lift heavy objects. And the suits frequently need recharging. But fifty years from now, Quinlivan thinks it could be possible to make one Iron-Man-style suit that assists with everything.

TINKERING WITH BIOLOGY

People of the future may not have to wear machinery or clothing to gain superpowers. They may also change their own biology. People can already enhance their body's abilities if they exercise, eat, and sleep well. Sports stars take this to the extreme, following strict diet and training regimens. Athletes who want a shortcut may turn to drugs to boost performance. This is called 'doping'. It is illegal and a form of cheating—yet it is still widespread in sport.

Most of the time, doping means adding extra hormones to the body. Hormones are chemicals that the body produces in order to send messages. It's natural for some hormones to tell muscles to grow bigger and stronger. But doping adds unnaturally high amounts of these hormones and spreads

> **Doping means adding extra hormones to the body.**

them throughout the entire body. Athletes who take hormones risk developing harmful side effects, including liver or heart damage. Those who organize and manage sports work hard to prevent doping. They punish athletes who do it by banning or suspending them from the sport. E. Paul Zehr is a neuroscientist at the University of Victoria and author of the book *Chasing Captain America: How Advances in Science, Engineering and Biotechnology Will Produce a Superhuman*. He says that performance-enhancing drugs are "like a giant hammer being used to chisel a very small thing."

Could there be a safer, more precise way to improve ourselves? Yes. We could change our genes. As we learned in Chapter 7, genes tell living cells how to grow and what to do. Genetic engineering technology deliberately alters genes to change how a living thing develops. This technology works on mushrooms, mammoths, and people, too. Sometimes, a mistake in the genes either causes a disease or makes a person more likely to develop a disease. Gene editing can fix a mistake in the genes of a single cell. But a body with a genetic disorder has copied that mistake into the genes of each and every cell. "You can't go edit all 40 trillion cells in the body," says Samuel Sternberg, a biochemist at Columbia University.

Thankfully, for many disorders, the edit only needs to be made in the part of the body that is unwell.

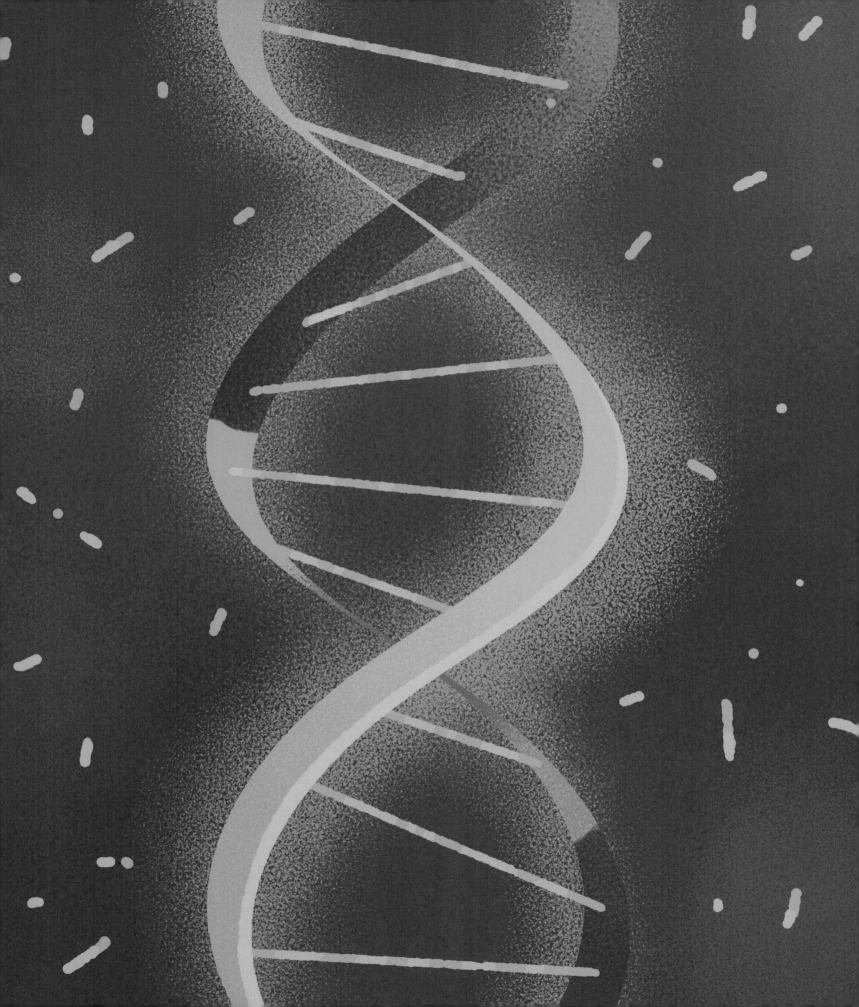

One way to do this is to remove a few cells from a person's body, edit them, then put them back. The altered cells then multiply and replace the old cells. Doctors call this gene therapy. They are already using it to treat a few specific medical conditions. Every form of gene therapy must go through careful research and testing to make sure it will be safe and effective.

In 2015, doctors got permission to try gene therapy on a one-year old named Layla Richards. She had leukemia, a type of cancer. Doctors engineered cells to seek and destroy the leukemia cells while leaving her normal body cells alone. Then they injected the cells into the baby's body. The treatment saved her life. In 2019, gene therapy cured a blood disorder called sickle cell disease in Victoria Gray, a 34-year-old mother from Mississippi.

PLAYING WITH FIRE

The same technology that cured these people could someday alter human life as we know it. Researchers could find ways to edit genes to make people stronger or faster, or even to increase their intelligence. They could make some of these changes in adults. But the most straightforward way to spread a genetic change throughout an entire body is to edit an embryo before it develops into a baby. The changes will automatically get copied into every single cell as the fetus grows. There's a huge risk to this type of procedure, though. If a gene-edited child ever has children of their own, they could inherit the changes, then pass them down to their children, and so on. Altering one embryo could change the evolutionary future of the entire human species!

Researchers could find ways to edit genes to make people stronger or faster, or even to increase their intelligence.

It doesn't help matters that the best tool for editing genes, CRISPR, is not a word processing program that can cleanly remove or replace parts of the genetic code. Dr. Kiran Musunuru, a doctor at the University of Pennsylvania, explains, "I think of it like fire. If you control fire, you can cook food or keep warm. But if you don't have good control, it can do very bad things." Using CRISPR is sort of like using a match to burn out just one paragraph of a book of instructions. Even the best doctor or engineer could accidentally burn other parts of the book, too. This could cause unintended changes to the genes. That may be an acceptable risk when you're doing gene therapy on a child or adult whose life is already at risk from an illness. But it's a very alarming risk in an embryo.

Doctors already make embryos in the lab for parents who can't get pregnant on their own. They extract sperm and eggs, join them together in the lab, and implant one or more embryos in the mother. Almost all scientists and governments agree that it's still too dangerous to implant gene-edited embryos. But the Chinese scientist He Jiankui did it anyway, sparking outrage around the world. His goal was to add resistance to the disease HIV, but his edits didn't work out as planned. "The editing was wild and uncontrolled. It was a disaster," says Musunuru. Jiankui's experiment led to the birth of twin girls, nicknamed Lulu and Nana, in October 2018. Jiankui was sent to jail, but the damage was already done. It's not yet known whether the twins or any of their descendants will suffer because of the experiment. But they could, and that risk was not worth taking.

It's still too dangerous to implant gene-edited embryos.

DESIGNER BABIES

Scientists will likely find safer, more controlled ways to edit the genes in embryos. When that happens, gene editing could protect children from inheriting a deadly disease or painful condition. This could prevent suffering. But how do we draw the line between an edit that's medically necessary and one that's not? For example, in 2019 a Russian couple learned that any child they had would inherit two copies of a gene that causes hearing loss or deafness. They were considering using gene editing to allow them to have a hearing child. It may seem reasonable for the couple to make that choice, as long as the procedure is safe. But many people belong to a thriving Deaf culture with its own language and history. Some already reject cochlear implants, because they feel like deafness is not something that should be fixed. Gene editing is yet another threat to their culture.

People with blindness, autism, or intellectual disabilities may also feel that they don't need fixing. In many cases, the very thing that makes someone different also allows that person to contribute to society in a unique way. Some blind people have learned how to navigate the world through echolocation. Some people with autism are brilliant musicians or mathematicians. If parents of the future can choose to avoid conditions such as these, we could end up with a less diverse world, or a world in which harassment of people who aren't considered "normal" is even more widespread than it is today.

> How do we draw the line between an edit that's necessary and one that's not?

Science fiction writers have imagined a future in which parents select all the traits they want their child to have, from hair and eye color to intelligence and athletic ability. Parents may even be able to choose traits that don't naturally occur, such as enhanced vision or hearing or superhuman strength. However, scientists don't yet know how to edit intelligence, athletic ability, or most other personality traits. "We're nowhere close to being able to do that," says Musunuru. Something like athletic ability comes from the interaction of hundreds or even thousands of genes, plus a person's upbringing changes how genes turn on or off. So it may never be possible to edit genes to make a child good at music, sports, art, or math.

However, scientists do know of some simple genetic changes that could bestow specific traits. For example, deleting a single gene from the cells in an embryo causes an animal to develop much larger muscles than normal. Scientists have edited this gene to make cows, pigs, and sheep that look like four-legged bodybuilders. The edit would work on humans too, but for now, researchers are only focusing on edits that would prevent illness or suffering.

ENGINEERING NEW HUMANS

Soon, society will have to make some tough decisions about genetic and robotic enhancements that serve no medical purpose. Will we outlaw them? Tolerate them? Embrace them? It may seem obvious that we should seek to improve our bodies and minds. But people have done very evil things with the goal of "improving" humanity. Eugenics is a disturbing practice that seeks to prevent certain people from having children in order to remove their traits from the population. Eugenics has been used as a weapon against black people, mentally ill people, and other groups. We must keep this history in mind.

People have done evil things with the goal of "improving" humanity.

It's also important to remember that enhancements won't be available to everyone, especially not at first. New technology is usually very expensive, meaning that only rich and powerful people can afford it. The world is already unequal—wealthy people have better healthcare, better housing, more energy, and more opportunities. Enhanced genes would give them yet another advantage, which isn't fair. In fact, it seems a lot like cheating. In sports, we expect our favorite stars to work hard to become the best—not to take shortcuts. Shouldn't we expect the same of businesspeople, artists, students, and others? Lawrence Prograis would not look forward to a future in which people have superpowers. "I think it would make us all more unequal," he says.

However, there are some good arguments for human enhancements. Some day, people may never get sick thanks to special disease-resisting instructions in their genes. Rescue workers and firefighters could save more lives if they could move with superhuman speed, lift heavy debris, or withstand dangerous conditions. Doctors could help more people if they had superhuman vision or the ability to remain alert for emergencies at all hours. Astronauts could explore farther if they could withstand radiation and low gravity or breathe in a different atmosphere. If these types of enhancements existed, some people could use them to gain advantage over others. But if we have the technology to make humans healthier and more capable, then is it wrong to withhold that technology from the world, just because some might misuse it?

In the end, though, enhancement technology can't turn anyone into a perfect person. "The ideal human does not exist," says Prograis. "We are all constantly striving to become better humans." And many of the things we strive for, including kindness, understanding, and empathy, are traits that we have to learn through experience. It may be impossible to program them into someone's genes. We should also be wary of trying to fix things that don't need fixing. One of the wonderful things about humanity is how very different we all are.

MIND OVER MATTER

You're hanging out at home and you're bored. You wonder if your friend is busy. She has a swimming pool and it's a sweltering day.

As soon as the thought crosses your mind, you hear it repeated it back to you, as a message ready to send to your friend. "I'm bored. Want to go swimming?" You think the word "send," and away it goes. A moment later, you hear the tone that means you have a reply. You think the word "open" and hear the response inside your head. "Sure, come on over."

You have the power of telepathy. And it links you to so much more than just your friends. You're connected to the entire internet of things. Your house has been listening to your mental conversation. In response, it projects several swimsuit options into the space in front of you. You glance at one, and your closet spits out a swimsuit and towel, wrapped for travel. A tone in your head alerts you that a car is nearby and can stop to pick you up. You accept the ride with a single thought.

You're connected to the entire internet of things.

You're also connected to a vast treasure trove of human knowledge, experiences, and memories. Any fact you want to know comes to mind instantly, thanks to intelligent search engines. You can also record experiences as they happen and play them back anytime. On the ride over, you close your eyes and think, "play the funniest memory at the pool." Inside your head, you see a flock of ducks land in the pool and your friend's dog try to catch them. You weren't even there for this event—but your friend recorded it, so you can experience it too.

Now that your mind connects directly to any technology, you can access knowledge that far exceeds the capacity of your brain. You can experience things far beyond the limitations of your physical body and influence the world without moving a muscle. All you have to do is think.

SPARKS IN THE BRAIN

So how likely is this scenario? Amazingly, you can already control technology with your mind, thanks to something called a brain-computer interface, or BCI. The Emotiv and NeuroSky mind-controlled gaming systems came out in 2009. At the 2014 World Cup in Brazil, a man whose legs were paralyzed miraculously made the first kick of the game. He wore a robotic exoskeleton that he controlled with his thoughts. In 2016, students at the University of Florida raced flying drones with their minds.

Today's BCIs can't turn your thoughts into a text or record and replay memories, though. "We are still very, very far from being able to read what someone is thinking at any given moment," says John Chuang, an engineer at the University of California, Berkeley. But in the future, technology could advance to this point. Jack Gallant, a neuroscientist at the same university, says there's one big issue holding us back. "We can't measure the brain well enough," he says.

To understand mind-controlled technology, you must first know a little about how the brain works. That blob of gray stuff inside your skull contains hundreds of billions of cells called neurons. Each one has the ability to fire, or send out a spark of electricity. That spark will reach hundreds or even

Amazingly, you can already control technology with your mind.

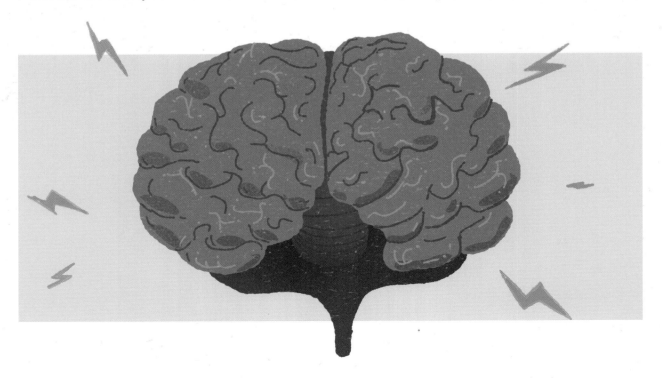

thousands of other neurons. Each of these may fire or not fire in response. Intricate patterns of firing neurons form all of your thoughts, emotions, movements, and physical sensations. (They also manage automatic processes that you aren't really aware of, such as breathing and keeping blood flowing throughout your body.) Your brain's patterns are consistent. Every time you raise your right hand, a bunch of neurons fire in pretty much the same way. Every time you see an apple, a different group of neurons fire. So if scientists can capture patterns of your neurons firing and match those patterns to specific actions (or images, or words, or whatever else they want to understand), then they can read your mind. Sound easy? It's not.

REAL TELEPATHY

Devices available today aren't able to detect the groups of neurons that fire to form thoughts.

The Emotiv, NeuroSky, and other similar devices available today can't detect the groups of neurons that fire to form specific thoughts or sensations. Why not? This is because they aren't close enough to the neurons. They read brain activity from outside the skull, through small metal sensors called electrodes. The electrodes nestle inside a cap, headband, or ear piece. From there, the device can capture the combined activity, called brainwaves, of many neurons in the brain.

A BCI that tracks brainwaves can tell whether you are awake or asleep, or whether your mind is calm or stressed. A BCI can also learn to recognize a certain pattern of brainwaves, then assign that pattern to an action in an app or game. For example, Chuang develops software that could soon allow people to set up "passthoughts" instead of passwords. To use the system, you first put on an electrode-studded earpiece. Then you think the same thought several times. For example, you could sing the chorus of a song inside your head. After a few repetitions, the device learns to recognize that pattern of brainwaves. Then, the next time it notices the same pattern, it will accept the passthought.

You would follow this same process to set up a mind-controlled gaming system. For example, you might imagine jumping. Once the system recognizes that thought pattern, you could jump in the game just by thinking. But you could just as easily think about swimming and use that thought to jump. The game doesn't know what the pattern means. It just matches the pattern to the action you assign it. In addition, a system like this can't separate your thoughts about singing a song or jumping from everything else happening in your brain. If you just had coffee or rode your bike, the device may no longer recognize your thoughts. "Anything else going on in the brain can get in the way," says Ana Matran-Fernandez, an engineer at the University of Essex who works on BCIs. The brain signals forming the energy boost from coffee or the mood boost from exercise would jumble together with the signals for the singing or jumping thought.

PEERING DEEPER

Trying to read a mind from outside the skull is like trying to follow a football game from outside the stadium.

Trying to read a mind from outside of the skull is like trying to follow a football game from outside of the stadium, says Matran-Fernandez. You can only hear the overall reaction of the crowd. Loud cheers or jeers could give you some idea of whether a team has scored. But you can't see or hear the individual players. So you can't learn much about what's actually going on in the game.

To read specific thoughts, researchers have to get closer to the action. "Somehow, you have to get into the brain," says Nicholas Hatsopoulos, a neuroscientist at the University of Chicago. That usually means surgery. Researchers have opened up the skulls of mice, rats, monkeys, and even some human volunteers to place tiny electrodes on or inside the brain. The people who choose to go through this type of surgery have a disease or disability that BCI technology may help treat.

Jan Schuermann was one of these volunteers. She has a rare disease which paralyzed her body from the neck down. Signals from her brain don't reach her arms or legs. In 2012, doctors placed two electrodes in her brain on the area that controls movement. Afterwards, metal posts stuck out of the top of her skull. Researchers could now link her movement-related brain signals to a computer. It took practice, but she learned to control a robot arm well enough to pick up a chocolate bar and take a bite. "It was the best chocolate ever," she recalls. She didn't have to think about the process. She just reached for the chocolate in the same way anyone would reach with a human arm, and the system responded.

The brain doesn't just send signals out to control the body. It also receives signals that it turns into a sense of touch and a sense of the body in space. Another volunteer, Scott Imbrie, is one of the first to feel touch through brain implants. A car accident left him partially paralyzed. He can walk and move his arms and hands, but his movements are limited. After brain surgery in 2020, he has two implants over the parts of his brain that sense touch in his right hand. When the research team sends electricity through the implants to the brain region that controls his thumb, he feels a prick there. Another two implants let him move a virtual arm in a simulation. "It's the coolest thing in the world," he says. "I feel like Doctor Octopus."

"I feel like Doctor Octopus."

For people who have lost limbs, brain surgery isn't always necessary. The brain sends and receives signals throughout the body using a web of nerves. Engineers can hijack this system by connecting a robot arm or leg directly to human bones, muscles, and nerves. Matt Carney designed a robotic foot and ankle as part of his PhD program at MIT. Patients have used their brains to swivel or tilt the foot. "It's sort of like an extension of your body," said Rebecca Mann, an amputee who has tried on the foot. Some people already use devices like this in their daily lives.

MIND MOVIES

Neuroscientists have hacked more than just the brain's movement and sensory systems. Medical implants that interface with the brain have restored basic hearing to the deaf and sight to the blind. Researchers have also begun to translate images and words from brain activity. Back in 2011, Gallant and his team at the University of California, Berkeley, reconstructed short, blurry videos from the brain activity of the people watching them. To avoid having to implant electrodes in or on the brain, they used an fMRI scanner, which tracks blood flow through the brain. In the future, results of experiments like these will keep getting clearer and clearer.

As we've already found out, caps and headbands don't capture very detailed brain activity. And an fMRI machine requires lying very still in a scanner, so wouldn't work for daily use. Invasive implants tend not to last long. This is because the body will start to attack the metal intruders or the surgery site may become infected. Scheurmann's had to be removed after just two years. But what if there were a better way to wire up the brain?

What if there were a better way to wire up the brain?

Elon Musk, the same inventor responsible for SpaceX, asked himself that same question. Then he started another company, Neuralink. It is working on something that Musk described as, "kind of like a Fitbit in your skull with tiny wires." A computer chip the size and shape of a large coin fits into a hole in the skull. Over a thousand tiny, thread-like electrodes hang from the chip down into the outer layer of the brain. These capture brain activity which the chip sends wirelessly to a nearby computer. In 2020, his team showed off a pig who had an implant capturing signals to her snout. It beeped whenever she sniffed. However, the team still has a lot of work to do to show the device is safe for human use.

BEWARE OF ZOMBIES

If we do find a safe and effective way to wire up our brains, then the scenario at the beginning of this chapter becomes possible. We'd no longer need to use our voices or hands to interface with our technology or with each other. But is this a future we really want?

As discussed in Chapter 8, wealthy people typically have access to new technology first. If having implants means thinking and working more rapidly and more smartly than people without implants, then it could become impossible for people to succeed in the world without them. This would widen the divide between rich and poor. Another thing to consider is that a telepathic connection to the world will not be a one-way street. Wireless devices and social media already allow you to reach out to anyone in the world at any time—which also means that anyone in the world can reach you at any time, unless you put all your gadgets away. What if ads, texts, funny dog videos, reminders, and more arrived directly in your brain? It could be maddening. "I wouldn't want to live in that world I think," says Matran-Fernandez.

Also, in order to allow mental texts or web searches or memory sharing, a BCI has to both read and write thoughts. This invasion of privacy would go far beyond any other technology humans have yet invented. Would you be able to choose which thoughts and memories the BCI can access? Will using the device cause brain damage or hamper your normal ability to think or remember? People might reprogram themselves to erase painful memories or even try out new personalities. Or police might use the technology to solve crimes and disputes by reading peoples' minds. Scarier still, a person hungry for power and control might hack into others' private thoughts and memories or even change them, turning the victims into brainwashed zombies. To prevent this, societies will have to decide what uses of this technology will be allowed and write laws to help protect people's rights.

What if ads, texts, and more arrived directly in your brain?

A BRAIN WITH NO BODY

The strangest thing about connecting our brains directly to our devices, though, might be the fact that this will change what it means to be human. Smart phones, watches, and tablets already act as extensions of the body and mind. You most likely rely on a device to get places, talk to people, and make basic decisions throughout the day. But today's devices can get lost in the couch cushions. A BCI that sits inside your skull probably wouldn't feel like a gadget—it would feel like part of your mind. You wouldn't have a phone anymore. You would be the phone. Imbrie said that when he uses his implants, "it's like I have a third arm." What if we all had as many arms, eyes, ears, or other senses as we wanted at any time? We'd live our lives very differently.

Some people have wondered whether we may someday upload our entire minds into computer systems. Then we could become immortals who inhabit bodies only when we want to, if at all. In a 2018 interview, futurist Ray Kurzweil predicted that this will begin happening by the 2030s, saying, "People will think it pretty primitive that back in 2018, people only had one body and they couldn't back up their mind file." If human minds are ever freed from biological bodies, we could more easily explore the solar system and beyond. We wouldn't have to put up with pain, aging, hunger, or disease. We could potentially live forever, almost as gods and goddesses. But would you want to? Chapter 6 explored some of the reasons that living forever might not be so great. The lack of a body makes the situation even weirder. Even if you interacted with the world through robotic sensors, it wouldn't be the same. Much of our joy in life comes from eating, exercising, hugging, sleeping, and more activities that require bodies. It's hard to imagine life without any of these things.

We have no evidence that total mind uploads will ever be possible.

We have no evidence that total mind uploads will ever be possible. But direct links between technology and the mind already exist and will improve over time. If BCIs get to the point where you can share ideas or dreams or memories directly with others, you may lose track of which were yours to begin with. People could certainly misuse this power. But it's also possible that the technology could allow people to understand each other and their world more completely and more deeply than ever before. Imagine a mother and son temporarily sharing minds during an argument so they can see things from the other's point of view. Perhaps, this could erase some of the issues that divide humanity and help to bring everyone closer together.

A WORLD AWARE

You smile as you watch the sun set over the ocean. At the same time, you're measuring rainfall on the other side of the world, assembling products at thousands of factories, directing an adventure movie about pirates, and so much more.

You can do all of this because you are not really human. You have a human body, but your mind is something spectacular. Implants in your brain continually communicate with every other human mind in the entire world to share and download experiences, ideas, knowledge, and understanding. All of these implants also connect to sensors placed throughout the world in natural environments, buildings, robots, and devices. These sensors constantly collect data of all kinds so that you can see, hear, smell, touch, taste, and remember anything that happens, anywhere in the world.

This torrent of information would overwhelm a normal human brain. Thankfully, your implants

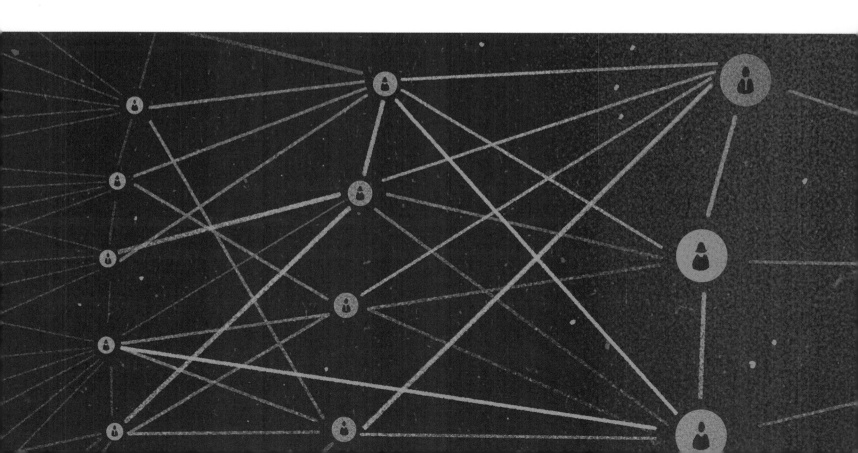

You can do all of this because you are not really human.

also connect to powerful supercomputers that process and store all the information. This vast interconnected system of brains, sensors, and computers has astounding intelligence and power. Plus, the system constantly learns, improving itself and becoming more intelligent over time. It has become a new kind of mind, with a sense of consciousness unlike anything a regular, singular human could ever experience. Your body and brain are merely one small part of what has become known as the World Mind.

Every day, the World Mind churns out new inventions. It cures diseases, finds new ways of making things, builds new robots and other machines, and even creates new forms of art, music, drama, and sport. It has slowly reversed climate change, backing Earth away from the brink of environmental disaster. The ocean you're watching is filled with glaciers and thriving sea life again. The World Mind protects all the animals and plants in the world and has found ways to make and distribute food, clothing, and shelter so that no one experiences poverty. It has built and launched starships to explore the galaxy. It has also established societies and governments that keep everyone at peace. War belongs to the distant past.

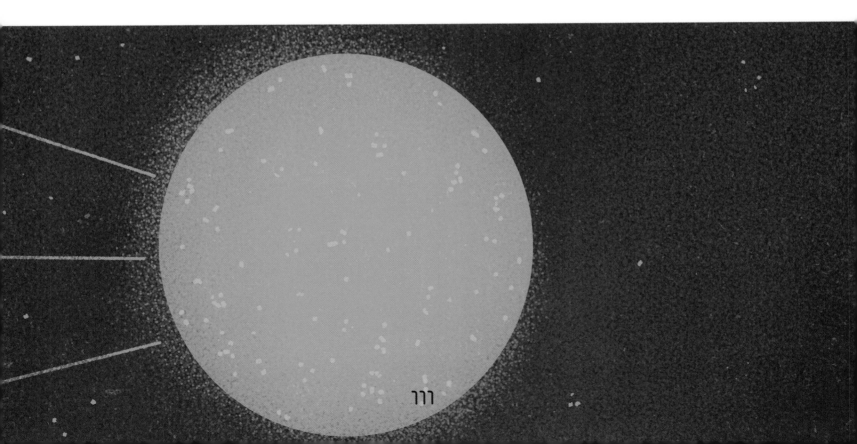

The World Mind is a superintelligence, a form of artificial intelligence (AI) that greatly exceeds the capabilities of a regular human brain.

THE SINGULARITY

A superintelligence such as the World Mind would drastically change humanity and the planet (or planets) that we call home. In this future, would you have a sense of self and purpose that is separate from other people's? Or would you be one cog in a mighty machine that runs everything? No one knows. Futurists have a special name for the arrival of a technology like the World Mind: the singularity. The singularity is an event that changes everything so drastically that it's impossible to know now what life will be like beyond that point.

The famous computer scientist Ray Kurzweil has imagined that when the singularity arrives, people will merge with their superintelligent machines, becoming computer-human hybrids, or even bodiless minds, as we discussed in Chapter 9. This could mark the extinction of human life, or the beginning of a new and improved form of humanity, depending on how you look at it. Kurzweil thinks the singularity will happen by 2045, but his is an extreme view. Most AI researchers think it could be many decades, centuries, or even longer before it's possible to create (or become) a superintelligence. Some think we will never get there.

Humans and machines are already joining forces.

However, humans and machines are already joining forces to increase their intelligence. We carry phones, tablets, and smart watches with us everywhere and sleep with them beside our pillows. "While it's not yet inside our bodies and brains, it may as well be," Kurzweil says, "because we don't dare leave home without it. It really is an extension of our minds." Apps and the internet bestow us with near-perfect maps, knowledge of the weather, and so much more. Often, people don't think much about internet access until it's interrupted. Like electricity, it's supposed to always be there, anywhere we go. Access has become a basic human right, according to the United Nations.

Meanwhile, humans are gathering and creating data at a staggering rate. At the beginning of 2020, the number of bytes of data in all our computers was estimated to be 40 times larger than the number of stars in the observable universe! And we're creating quintillions of bytes of new data every single day. All that data only helps, though, if we use it wisely. Intelligence is the ability to respond to information by taking action or solving a problem. Computer programs, also called algorithms or models, can churn through data much faster and more efficiently than human brains. AI models make decisions or take action based on data. Today, AI models drive cars, serve up search results, diagnose disease, translate languages, and much more. Just how smart is AI now? And could it ever become vastly smarter than humans?

COMPUTER OVERLORDS

Could AI ever become vastly smarter than humans?

Artificial intelligence has come a long way. In the 1950s, computers the size of a large room processed several thousand instructions per second. Today, an Apple Bionic phone fits in your pocket and processes 5 trillion instructions per second. As the capacity and speed of computers increases, researchers develop ever smarter programs. Some surpass human ability at specific tasks. In 1997, the IBM supercomputer Deep Blue defeated the human chess champion, Gary Kasparov. In 2011, another computer called Watson won the game show *Jeopardy!* And in 2017, AlphaGo, an AI model developed by Google's AI company, DeepMind, conquered a game called Go. (Go is a strategy game like chess, but with many more possible moves on each turn.)

These were all exciting moments for AI. After losing to Watson at *Jeopardy!*, Ken Jennings wrote: "I, for one, welcome our new computer overlords." But don't worry, this was a joke. Computers are brilliant at storing heaps of information and processing it rapidly. But computers still miss out on an important component of human intelligence: understanding. AI models are still programs that follow instructions. Watson can't turn against humans and become an overlord any more than a toaster could suddenly decide to freeze bread instead of heating it.

BRUTE FORCE

Watson and all the other intelligent systems we have today are examples of narrow AI. This kind of technology can only do one job, often in very specific conditions. It uses the brute force of its memory and speed to accomplish a task. Deep Blue searched through 20 to 40 billion possible future states of the chess board, searching for moves that were most likely to lead towards a win. Watson quickly combed through encyclopedias, Wikipedia pages, and other reference material—equivalent to about one million books! Then it calculated which words or phrases seemed most likely to answer the question. AlphaGo played nearly five million games of Go against itself to learn how to win.

AlphaGo's success relied on a new AI technique called deep learning. Deep learning doesn't mean the computer understands anything deeply. The name refers to the size of something called an artificial neural network (ANN). This is a type of AI model with a structure inspired by the human brain. Like a brain, an ANN can learn from experience.

Deep learning models rely on very large and complex ANNs. And they must learn, or train, on huge amounts of data. To learn to recognize images, a deep learning model first looks at millions of images each labeled with a name. If it has enough examples, it can figure out the shapes and colors that tend to go with a label like 'dog,' or 'mermaid' or 'cow.' Then when it sees a dog that isn't labeled, it will recognize what it is.

Deep learning has vastly improved computers' ability to identify images, recognize faces, translate languages, grasp objects, design new medicines, and much more. "So far, we haven't run out of areas where we can apply these pattern matching, data-crunching algorithms," says Andrey Kurenkov, who is researching AI and robotics at Stanford University. Deep learning is amazing technology. But it doesn't match the abilities of a human mind. For example, DeepMind also designed an AI model to play the video game Breakout. The game involves moving a little paddle from side to side in order to bounce a ball and break bricks at the top of the screen. Impressively, the system came up with a strategy of making a tunnel through the bricks that helped it reach higher scores than most people. But if the paddle moved up just a few pixels on the screen, the model could no longer win. Why was that?

> The system came up with a strategy of making a tunnel through the bricks.

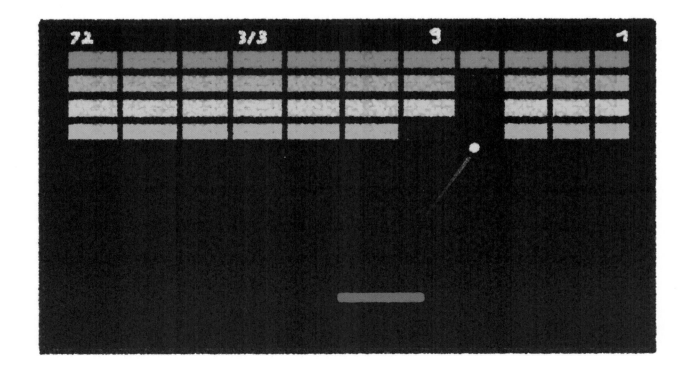

KANGAROOS AND MER-COWS

The algorithm couldn't adapt, even to such a tiny change, because it didn't understand the game. "It had not learned the same concepts that we humans use to play this game," explains Melanie Mitchell, an AI researcher at the Santa Fe institute. If you played Breakout only once, you would grasp the general purpose of the ball, paddle, and bricks and that the game involves bouncing one thing into some other things. You could play the game even if the paddle became a kangaroo bouncing a pineapple off its tail to change the colors of floating bubbles. Today's AI systems can't adapt the things they learn to new situations.

Today's AI systems can't adapt the things they learn to new situations.

You also don't need millions of examples of something to learn a new concept. In fact, you may only need one example in order to recognize a new idea in the future: Imagine a mer-cow. Got an image of it in your mind? You can use imagination and common sense to visualize this wacky creature. A brand new AI system named DALL-E could generate a mermaid-cow image, thanks to a combination of image and language processing algorithms. (It managed to draw pictures of an avocado arm chair and a giraffe-turtle!) But most computers and robots can't handle such surprising ideas or situations. And the real world is filled with surprises, as we learned in Chapter 1.

Engineers can use virtual simulations to train robots and other machines that have to interact with the real world. But even in a simulation, it's impossible to predict every type of situation that may occur. Take self-driving cars as an example. These cars exist, but a human almost always has to sit in the driver's seat, ready to take over if needed. The cars usually only drive on well-known roads in good weather conditions. Yann LeCun is an AI expert at Facebook who developed the first deep learning systems in the 1990s. He points out that if engineers let one of today's AI models loose to train itself to drive a

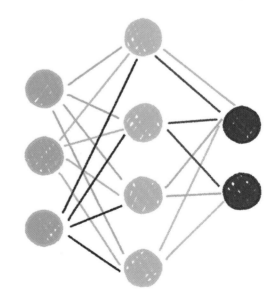

car, it would have to drive for millions of hours and crash into thousands of trees, houses, animals, people, road signs, and more before it learned to identify and avoid these obstacles. And it still wouldn't know what to do if it came across a couch in the middle of the road! "This does not reflect the learning animals and humans do," LeCun said. "There's something missing."

common sense

We use common sense to understand the world around us.

What's missing is common sense. This includes all the knowledge people never talk about because it's so obvious. We use common sense to understand the world around us, predict what will happen next, and to come up with reasons for things that already happened. Long before you try to drive a car, you understand that running into solid things at high speed is a bad idea. You also know that things fall down when they aren't supported. String can pull on something but not push on it. A solid container can hold liquid. And so on. Computers don't know any of this.

A lack of common sense doesn't just impact self-driving cars. It's also the main reason why virtual assistants and robots have such trouble with human language. People tend to leave out obvious, common-sense information when they talk. Since this information is not at all obvious to machines, they still can't read and understand text or hold a meaningful conversation. If you try talking to a virtual assistant such as Siri or Alexa, you'll notice that it often says strange or irrelevant things. A robot or virtual assistant with common sense would have a much easier time conversing.

People learn some common-sense concepts as babies and very young children. But the most basic level of common sense is with us (and many other animals) from birth. Even newborn chicks understand that an object that moves out of view still exists. Mitchell points out, "It is still a grand challenge in AI to get a machine that has the common sense of an 18-month-old baby."

Perhaps the brute force of faster, more powerful computers or more complex deep learning models will solve this problem. But many experts think that's unlikely. 'We're missing some basic insights,' says Gary Marcus, co-founder of the company Robust.AI. AI developers will likely have to build

innate, common-sense concepts into computer systems, or find a way for computers to learn these concepts on their own, he says. Most likely, developers will have to invent new AI techniques. This could make possible strong AI, also called artificial general intelligence.

AN INTELLIGENCE EXPLOSION

When artificial general intelligence that can understand language and grasp real-world situations arrives, incredible opportunities will open up. This strong AI would merge the human ability to reason and understand with the ability to remember and analyze huge amounts of information at incredible speeds. Approximately 2.5 million pieces of research are published every year, which is over 5,000 each day. No single person can keep up with all of this knowledge. This slows down the pace of discovery since human scientists, doctors, and other experts often miss out on each other's work.

No single person can keep up with all of this knowledge.

A computer can easily read millions of research papers. If it could understand them, too, it could speed up the development of new technology, the discovery of new drugs, and so much more. It could tackle problems in law, government, and the environment. It could greatly increase humanity's ability to accomplish things. "I think that at some point AI will fundamentally transform science and technology and medicine," says Marcus. "It's going to be phenomenal."

"With artificial intelligence, we're summoning the demon."

Ultimately, though, humans may lose control over a strong intelligence. Elon Musk famously said, "With artificial intelligence, we're summoning the demon." Why might a strong AI be dangerous? The best way to create one may be to build a system that can improve itself. Once a self-improving system exists, it could potentially make itself so smart that people can no longer understand or control it. We'd be powerless to stop it from accomplishing its goals, whatever they may be. This could be a problem even if the AI doesn't seek to harm humans. For example, people are much smarter than frogs. We don't want to hurt frogs—we just don't really care what they do. But if we needed to build a new road and it went through a frog pond, most of us wouldn't think twice about building that road. The frogs would have no way to stop us or prepare for what would be about to happen to them. When it comes to superintelligent AI, we're the frogs.

One key to AI development is making sure that its goals match our own—in other words, it must always care about the frogs and take their needs and desires into account. Giving a machine a sense of right and wrong isn't a simple problem. Thankfully, organisations such as the Partnership on Artificial Intelligence are thinking about these issues and developing guidelines for trustworthy AI.

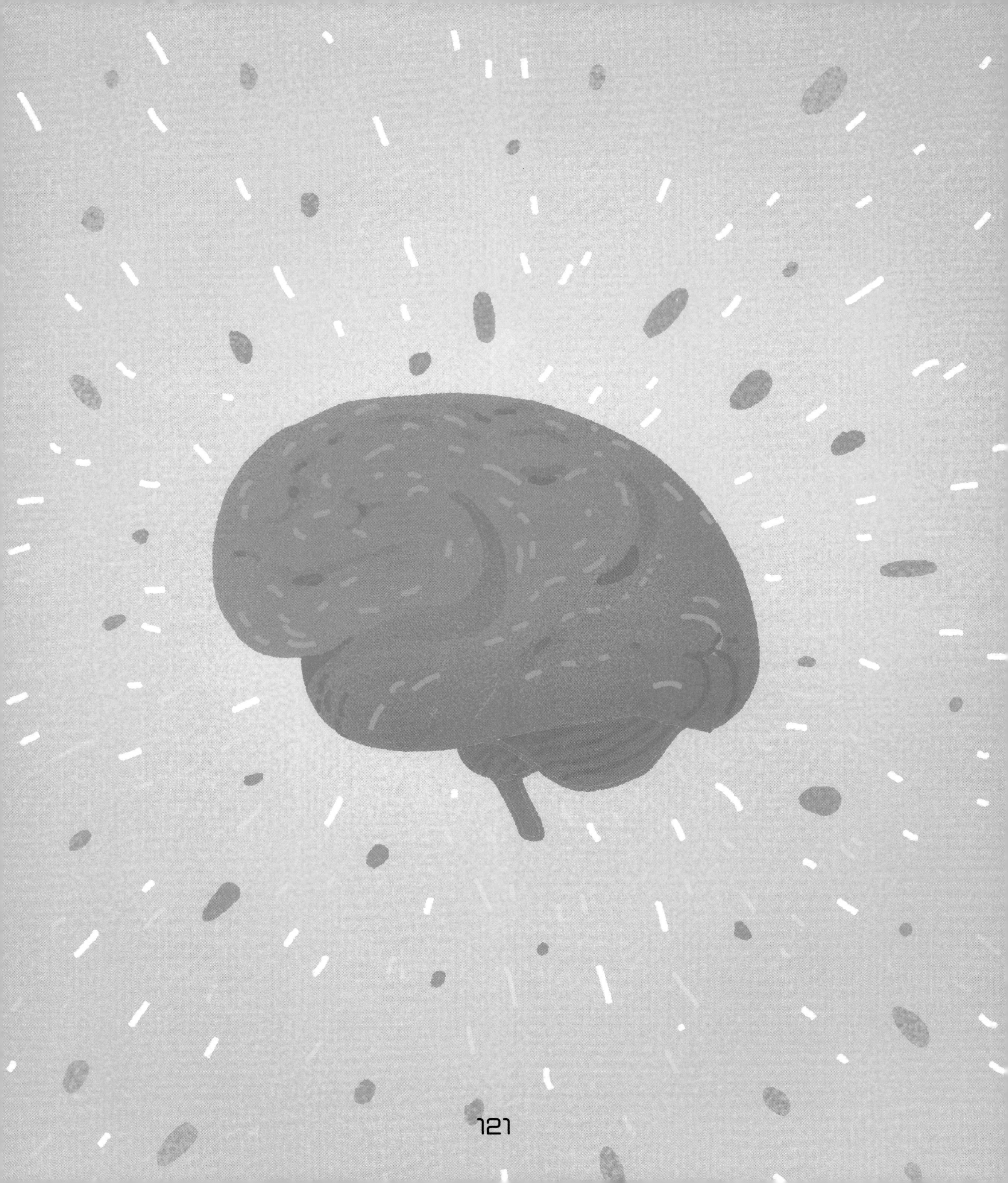

THE RISKS OF AI

AI can learn and maintain human biases.

Even if we never develop superintelligent AI, the narrow AI we already have comes with serious risks. AI allows us to do anything more efficiently and intelligently—and that includes terrible tasks such as killing or controlling people. World leaders could create smart weapons that know how to hide themselves or how to choose very specific targets. Activists are already working to prevent the development of these types of weapons. AI could be used for surveillance as well. A government could set up an AI-powered system that watches people every moment of the day, rewarding those who follow rules and punishing those who don't.

Another danger is far more subtle. AI can learn and maintain human biases. For example, some software trained to recognize faces can't identify dark-skinned faces as easily as light-skinned ones. Why? The data is biased. Developers usually train their models on vast collections of online images that tend to contain more light-skinned faces. A police department or airport using this model might detain people who did nothing wrong, just because the model misidentified them. That's unfair and racist.

It should lift up humanity-all of humanity.

How do we avoid harmful bias in AI? Ayanna Howard, a roboticist and dean of the college of engineering at The Ohio State University, says, "we need to have diverse voices contributing." When people of a variety of races, nationalities, genders, socioeconomic classes, and ages work together to create new technology, they each bring unique perspectives and experiences to the design process. The result is technology that is truly for everyone. "If we become better humans, the AI we create will become better, too," says Howard.

TECHNOLOGY FOR THE GOOD OF ALL

Working together to improve ourselves and the technology we create is important not only in AI, but in all areas of technology. Remember that technology is a tool and it's up to us to use it for the

right purposes. What are those purposes? Not everyone has the same ideas about right and wrong. But there are some points we can all agree on. Beneficial technology makes it easier for us to live healthy lives, learn, discover, explore, understand each other, and express ourselves. It should lift up humanity—all of humanity—not just those with money and power.

The development of any of the futuristic technologies explored in this book would transform the world (and possibly the entire universe) in strange and unpredictable ways. But we have to try to imagine what might happen. We can only prepare for a future that we've considered in advance.

So we must stretch our imaginations, wonder, and dream. Then we have to get to work researching, experimenting, and speaking up for our values. You and every young person out there will be the ones to decide what to do with all the amazing technology humanity is developing. The future is in your hands. What will you do with it?

END NOTES

I spoke with over fifty experts during the research for this book! I'm grateful to every single one of them for sharing their ideas about the future. You can find a selection of complete interviews on my website, kathrynhulick.com.

Chapter 1: Robots Everywhere

Thank you to Michael Gennert for taking me on a tour of the robotics labs at WPI.

p. 10 "I think we will," Ross Hatton. Personal Interview, July 18, 2019.

p. 11 "Imagine trying to..." Michael Gennert. Personal Interview, August 2, 2019.

p. 11 A person can pick up between 400 and 600 items per hour. Goldberg's robots have achieved 500 picks per hour for simple shapes, but just 300 picks per hour for more complex objects. Ken Goldberg. Personal Interview. August 1, 2019.

p. 14 Scheutz points out... Matthias Scheutz. Personal Interview, August 14, 2019. Watch the demonstration: HRILaboratory. Simple Natural Language Interaction with Consequence Reasoning. YouTube, August 3, 2015. www.youtube.com

p. 15 "I think the ideas we see..." Elizabeth Hunter, Rebecca Li, and Jimmy Paulos. Personal Interview, July 25, 2019.

p. 16 A smart home filled with sensors... Kathryn Hulick. "Greening your digital life." Science News for Students, March 25, 2021.

p. 16 People could end up homeless... Martin Ford. *Rise of the Robots: Technology and the Threat of a Jobless Future.* Basic Books, 2016.

p. 17 Only if people get the right materials... and p. 19 A person who yells at a robot assistant... and p. 122 "We need to have diverse voices..." Ayanna Howard. Personal Interview, December 15, 2020.

p. 19 People who use robots like Paro... Sherry Turkle. *Alone Together: Why We Expect More from Technology and Less from Each Other.* Basic Books, 2012.

p. 19 Isaac Asimov. "Runaround," *I, Robot.* Doubleday, 1963.

p. 19 The art shows the robots Paro (top left) and Pepper (bottom right).

p. 19 Unfortunately, rules like these... Kathryn Hulick. "Teaching robots right from wrong." *Science News for Students*, April 20, 2017.

Chapter 2: Teleportation

Further Reading: Jeremy Bailenson. *Experience on Demand: What Virtual Reality Is, How It Works, and What It Can Do.* W. W. Norton & Company, 2018.

p. 22 According to scientists... Lawrence Krauss. *The Physics of Star Trek.* Basic Books, 2007.

p. 23 Researchers have calculated... David Starkey. "To infinity and beyond: teleporting humans into space." University of Leicester, July 30, 2013. www2.le.ac.uk

p. 23 It's actually possible to instantly teleport very small amounts of information using quantum entanglement. Learn about it: Jesse Emspak. "Chinese Scientists Just Set the Record for the Farthest Quantum Teleportation." LiveScience, July 14, 2017.

p. 25 "It literally looks like a real flower..." and p. 31 "Who you are..." Nima Zeighami. Personal Interview, September 24, 2019.

p. 26 "The robot mimics head movement." Emre Tanirgan. Personal Interview, October 23, 2019.

p. 27 "We don't just think with our minds..." and p. 30 "You can go anywhere..." Toshi Anders Hoo. Personal Interview, September 9, 2019.

p. 28 Jang Ji-sung and Nayeon's story: Kyle Melnick. "VR Technology Reunites Grieving Mother With Her Deceased Child." VRScout, February 8, 2020. vrscout.com

p. 28 "So I can 'be with' my family..." Liv Erickson. Personal Interview, November 2020.

Chapter 3: Cities in Space

p. 34 In 1969, President Richard Nixon considered this plan by the chief architect of the rocket that made the moon landing possible: Wernher Von Braun, "Manned Mars Landing: Presentation to the Space Task Group." August 4, 1969. www.nasa.gov

p. 34 Rocket propellant and payload costs: Kelly and Zach Weinersmith. *Soonish.* Penguin Press, 2017. This book also has an excellent section on space elevators. These could someday carry people into space instead of rockets.

p. 35 Elon Musk predicts a 2026 Mars landing and p. 42 "I think it's important..." Elon Musk. "Axel Springer Award 2020." YouTube, streamed live on December 1, 2020. www.youtube.com

p. 35 "We have the technology..." Brooke Grindlinger, et al. "What Will it Take to Bring Humans to Mars?" The New York Academy of Sciences, virtual panel presentation, May 12, 2020.

p. 36 "Yesterday's coffee..." John Schwartz. "Water Flowing From Toilet to Tap May Be Hard to Swallow" *The New York Times*, May 8, 2015. www.nytimes.com

p. 37 "will live most of their lives..." Robert Zubrin. Personal Interview, August 12, 2019.

p. 38 "When it cools down..." and p. 42 "Our future cannot be limited..." Berok Khoshnevis. Personal Interview, August 15, 2019.

p. 38 "These threads..." and p. 40 "It's actually the most Earth-like..." Jason Derleth. Personal Interview, August 22, 2019.

p. 38 Fungus structures: Lynn Rothschild. "Astrobiology & Growing Things in Space." Techfestival 2018, October 19, 2018, Copenhagen.

p. 39 Alternatively, you could... Mike Wall. "Looks Like Elon Musk Is Serious About Nuking Mars." Space.com, August 21, 2019. www.space.com

p. 39 In 2018, NASA scientists calculated... Bill Steigerwald and Nancy Jones. "Mars Terraforming Not Possible Using Present-Day Technology." NASA Goddard Space Flight Center, July 30, 2018. www.nasa.gov

p. 39 "a fixer-upper..." "Elon Musk on Mars: 'It's a fixer-upper of a planet'" CBS News, September 21, 2012. www.cbsnews.com

p. 40 The illustration is based on art made by Rick Guidice for NASA Ames Research Center in the 1970s.

p. 40 Learn about the effort underway to send light sail spacecraft to Alpha Centauri: Zac Manchester. "How Do You Fly to Alpha Centauri in Just 20 Years? Ride a Laser Beam." *IEEE Spectrum*, June 6, 2016. spectrum.ieee.org

p. 42 "What if when we go..." Danielle Wood. Personal Interview, December 9, 2020. For more on avoiding the mistakes of colonialism in space exploration: Danielle Wood. "On Indigenous People's Day, Let's Commit to an Anticolonial Mindset on Earth and in Space." MIT Media Lab, October 12, 2020. www.media.mit.edu

p. 43 "Earth is home..." and "How do we want..." Lucianne Walkowicz. Personal Interview, August 21, 2019.

Chapter 4: Endless Clean Energy

Further reading: Daniel Clery. *A Piece of the Sun: The Quest for Fusion Energy*. Abrams Press, 2013.

p. 46 "Who wouldn't want to..." Saskia Mordijck. Personal Interview, August 7, 2019.

p. 48 The ideal fusion fuel is a mix of two forms of hydrogen called deuterium and tritium. Deuterium is found in seawater. And tritium is made from lithium, which can also be found in sea water.

p. 50 "We are the hottest place..." and "It will be a huge celebration." Tammy Ma. Personal Interview, August 7, 2019.

p. 50 Learn about ITER: www.iter.org

p. 50 Over the past century, average temperatures on Earth have risen over 1 degree Celsius. That may not seem like a lot, but it really matters. See: Rebecca Lindsey and LuAnn Dahlman. "Climate Change: Global Temperature." Climate.gov, March 15, 2021. www.climate.gov

p. 50 Fusion scientists is the US plan to build... and p. 53 "It's a race against time." Arturo Dominguez. Personal Interviews, August 6, 2019 and January 11, 2021.

p. 53 The IPCC's report on climate change: "Summary for Policymakers of IPCC Special Report on Global Warming of 1.5°C approved by governments." IPCC, October 8, 2018. www.ipcc.ch

p. 53 New nuclear fission power plants: Isabella Isaccs-Thomas. "How the Next Generation of Nuclear Reactors Could Be Smaller, Greener and Safer." PBS News Hour, February 12, 2020. www.pbs.org

p. 55 "help poor countries..." and "we need a lot of miracles..." Rose Mutiso. Personal Interview, January 15, 2021.

Chapter 5: Food For All

p. 58 This talk helped launch the field of nanotechnology: Richard P. Feynman. "There's Plenty of Room at the Bottom." California Institute of Technology Journal of Engineering and Science, Volume 23, February 1960.

p. 58 In the nano-scale world... and "seems a futuristic fantasy." Simone Schuerle. Personal Interview, October 17, 2019.

p. 59 The cotton-growing research won a Global Change Award in 2020. globalchangeaward.com

p. 59 "If you want a table..." Quoted in Daniel Ackerman. "Could lab-grown plant tissue ease the environmental toll of logging and agriculture?" MIT News Office, January 20, 2021. news.mit.edu

p. 60 Thank you to Matthew Ball and The Good Food Institute for assisting with information about plant-based and cell-based meat.

p. 60 "What you have at the end..." M.J. Kinney. Personal Interview, September 10, 2019.

p. 63 Some professional runners already get shoes 3D printed specially for them. People have already 3D printed guitars with intricate shapes, wheelchairs for cats and dogs, cakes with secret messages hidden inside, replicas of prehistoric fossils, and so much more.

p. 63 Berok Khoshnevis, the engineer who designed a way to 3D print on Mars, plans to use his equipment to make houses here on Earth. He says it will take just one day to print a complete house!

p. 63 Read more about shape-changing materials: Kelly and Zach Weinersmith. *Soonish*. Penguin Press, 2017.

p. 64 "It's close to meat..." Quoted in Henry Fountain. "Building a $325,000 Burger." *The New York Times*, May 12, 2013. www.nytimes.com

p. 66 "We need to find ways..." Quoted in Hod Lipson and Melba Kurman. *Fabricated: The New World of 3D Printing*. John Wiley & Sons, 2013.

Chapter 6: Living Forever

p. 69 "Advancements in science..." and p. 72 "Weiss predicts..." Dr. Daniel Weiss. Personal Interview, September 10, 2019.

p. 69 Statistics on human lifespans: Max Roser, et al. "Life Expectancy." Our World in Data, 2013. ourworldindata.org

p. 70 "Even though I have no heart..." Quoted in Peta Owens-Liston. "The First Artificial Heart, 30 Years Later." University of Utah Health, December 2, 2012. healthcare.utah.edu

p. 70 US organ donor statistics and sign up: www.organdonor.gov/statistics-stories/statistics.html

p. 71 Baboons with pig hearts: Jennifer Leman. "Baboons survive 6 months after getting a pig heart transplant." Science News, December 5, 2018. www.sciencenews.org

p. 72 Luke Massella's story: Padraig Belton. "'A new bladder made from my cells gave me my life back.'" BBC News, September 11, 2018. www.bbc.com

p. 72 "We're still very far..." Adam Feinberg. Personal Interview, September 26, 2019.

p. 73 The NASA Vascular Tissue Challenge: Jordan Miller. Personal Interview, October 9, 2019 and NASA. "STMD: Centennial Challenges." www.nasa.gov/vtchallenge

p. 74 "Doctors and scientists..." Dr. Saranya Wyles. Personal Interview, October 2, 2019.

p. 74 "Aging cannot be reversed." Robin Holliday. "Aging is No Longer an Unsolved Problem in Biology." Annals of the New York Academy of Sciences, Vol. 1067, May 1, 2006.

p. 75 Thank you to John Evans of the University of California San Diego for sharing his expertise on the ethics of longevity.

p. 76 "There comes a time..." and p. 98 "I think it would make us..." and p. 99 "The ideal human..." Lawrence Prograis. Personal Interview, February 9, 2021.

Chapter 7: Pet Dinosaurs

Further reading: Beth Shapiro. How to Clone a Mammoth: The Science of De-extinction. Princeton University Press, 2015.

p. 80 "No," and "the DNA was in terrible condition..." Beth Shapiro. Personal Interview, November 4, 2019.

p. 80 In 2021, Shapiro and a team of researchers reported sequencing DNA from mammoth teeth that were over a million years old! Ewen Callaway. "Million-year-old mammoth genomes shatter record for oldest ancient DNA." Nature, February 17, 2021. www.nature.com

p. 80 "Yes," and "We know we can..." and p. 84 "turn it on or turn it off..." and p. 87 "Every cool kind of dinosaur..." Jack Horner. Personal Interview, October 28, 2019.

p. 81 If you were to print the entire human genome... "How Will 'Cut And Paste' Technology Rewrite Our DNA?" TED Radio Hour, July 15, 2016. www.npr.org

p. 82 CRISPR/Cas9 is the complete name of the technology that earned Doudna and Charpentier a Nobel Prize. Most people shorten it to "CRIPSR."

p. 83 For updates on woolly mammoth restoration: "The Woolly Mammoth Revival: Progress to Date." Revive & Restore, https://reviverestore.org/projects/woolly-mammoth/progress/

p. 84 Hornless calves: Jef Akst. "Genetically Engineered Hornless Dairy Calves." The Scientist, May 10, 2016. www.the-scientist.com

p. 85 "eat less, but get all they need." Samuel Acheampong. Personal Interview, August 26, 2019.

p. 86 "I start to feel nervous." and p. 87 "If you're just putting horns..." Molly Hardesty-Moore. Personal Interview, October 23, 2019.

p. 86 Pleistocene park: Sergey A. Zimov. "Pleistocene Park: Return of the Mammoth's Ecosystem." Science, May 6, 2005. science.sciencemag.org

p. 86 "The hope is that someday..." Quoted in Amanpour & Company. "George Church Talks Age Reversal and Woolly Mammoth DNA." PBS, December 5, 2019. www.pbs.org

p. 86 How genetic engineering can help coral: Warren Cornwall. "Researchers embrace a radical idea: engineering coral to cope with climate change." Science, March 21, 2019. www.sciencemag.org

Chapter 8: Superpowers

Further reading: Jennifer A. Doudna and Samuel H. Sternberg. A Crack in Creation: Gene Editing and the Unthinkable Power to Control Evolution. Houghton Mifflin Harcourt, 2017.

p. 89 Supersuits were banned from professional swimming in 2010 because athletes who didn't wear them couldn't compete against those who did.

p. 90 "I returned to my sport stronger..." and p. 91 "Fifty years from now..." Hugh Herr quoted in Adam Piore. The Body Builders: Inside the Science of the Engineered Human. HarperCollins, 2017.

p. 90 Watch Markus Rehm's record jump: "Berlin 2018: Markus Rehm's record win." World Para Athletics, August 25, 2018. www.paralympic.org

p. 91 It could be possible to make one Iron-Man-style suit... Brendan Quinlivan. Personal Interview, September 27, 2019.

p. 92 "Like a giant hammer..." E. Paul Zehr. Personal Interview, October 16, 2019.

p. 92 "You can't go edit..." Samuel Sternberg. Personal Interview, November 3, 2019.

p. 94 Layla Richards' story: Sara Reardon. "Leukaemia success heralds wave of gene-editing therapies." Nature, November 5, 2015. www.nature.com

p. 94 Victoria Gray's story: Jocelyn Kaiser. "CRISPR and another genetic strategy fix cell defects in two common blood disorders." Science Magazine, December 5, 2020. www.sciencemag.org

p. 95 "I think of it like fire..." and "The editing was wild and uncontrolled..." and p. 97 "We're nowhere close..." Dr. Kiran Musunuru. Personal Interview, October 24, 2019.

p. 95 He Jiankui's experiment: Dennis Normile. "Chinese scientist who produced genetically altered babies sentenced to 3 years in jail." Science Magazine, December 30, 2019. www.sciencemag.org

p. 96 In 2019, a Russian couple learned… Jon Cohen. "Deaf couple may edit embryo's DNA to correct hearing mutation." Science Magazine, October 21, 2019. www.sciencemag.org. As of 2020, no family had used gene editing to prevent deafness. For more on the response from the Deaf community: Sarah Katz. "Why Deaf People Oppose Using Gene Editing To "Cure" Deafness." Discover, August 11, 2020. www.discovermagazine.com

Chapter 9: Mind Control

Further Reading: Miguel Nicolelis. *Beyond Boundaries: The New Neuroscience of Connecting Brains with Machines—and How it Will Change Our Lives.* Times Books, 2011.

p. 102 Mind-controlled drone race: Jason Dearn. "Mind-Controlled Drones Race to the Future." University of Florida Herbert Wertheim College of Engineering, April 28, 2016. www.eng.ufl.edu/

p. 102 "We are still very, very far…" and p. 103 Passthought research: John Chuang. Personal Interview, October 18, 2017.

p. 102 "We can't measure the brain…" Jack Gallant. Personal Interview, February 5, 2016.

p. 104 "Anything else going on in the brain…" and Trying to read a mind from outside the skull… and p. 107 "I wouldn't want to…" Ana Matran-Fernandez. Personal Interview, September 24, 2019.

p. 104 "Somehow, you have to get into the brain." Nicholas Hatsopoulos. Personal Interview, October 14, 2019.

p. 105 "It was the best chocolate ever." Jan Scheuermann. Personal Interview, February 17, 2016.

p. 105 "It's the coolest thing…" and p. 108 "It's like I have a third arm." Scott Imbrie. Personal Interview, January 26, 2021.

p. 105 Thank you to Matt Carney for showing me around his lab at MIT.

p. 105 "It's sort of like an extension…" Rebecca Mann, quoted in Mallika Marshall. "Brain-Controlled Bionic Limbs Developed At MIT." CBS Boston, December 17, 2018. boston.cbslocal.com

p. 106 Watch the movies reconstructed from brain signals: Yasmin Anwar. "Scientists use brain imaging to reveal the movies in our mind." Berkeley News, September 22, 2011. news.berkeley.edu

p. "Kind of like a fitbit…" Elon Musk in CNET "Watch Elon Musk's ENTIRE live Neuralink demonstration." YouTube, August 8, 2020. www.youtube.com

p. 108 Some experts have already proposed a set of "neurorights" to cover BCI technology: NeuroRights Initiative, https://nri.ntc.columbia.edu/

p. 108 "People will think it pretty primitive…" and p. 113 "While it's not yet inside…" Ray Kurzweil. "Ray Kurzweil on what the future holds next." The TED Interview, December 2018. www.ted.com

Chapter 10: A World Aware

Further Reading: Gary Marcus and Ernest Davis. *Rebooting AI: Building Artificial Intelligence We Can Trust.* Pantheon Books, 2019.

Melanie Mitchell. *Artificial Intelligence: A Guide for Thinking Humans.* Pelican Books, 2019.

Max Tegmark. *Life 3.0: Being Human in the Age of Artificial Intelligence.* Deckle Edge, 2017

p. 113 Kurzweil thinks this will happen by 2045… Christianna Reedy. "Kurzweil Claims That the Singularity Will Happen by 2045." Futurism, October 5, 2017. futurism.com

p. 114 By 2025, humans will be creating 100s of quintillions of bytes of data per day: Jeff Desjardins. "How much data is generated each day?" Visual Capitalist and World Economic Forum, April 17, 2019. www.weforum.org

p. 114 "I, for one, welcome…" John Markoff. "Computer Wins on 'Jeopardy!': Trivial, It's Not." *The New York Times*, February 16, 2011. www.nytimes.com

p. 116 "So far, we haven't run out of…" Andrey Kurenkov. Personal Interview, October 8, 2019.

p. 117 "It had not learned…" and p. 119 "It's still a grand challenge…" Melanie Mitchell. Personal Interview, February 10, 2020.

p. 117 Generate images with DALL-E: "DALL·E: Creating Images from Text." OpenAI, January 5, 2021. https://openai.com/blog/dall-e/

p. 118 "This does not reflect…" Yann LeCun in Lex Fridman (host). "Yann LeCun: Deep Learning, Convolutional Neural Networks, and Self-Supervised Learning (No. 36)." Lex Fridman Podcast, August 31, 2019. https://lexfridman.com/yann-lecun/

p. 118 Here's an example of a question that's obvious to humans but not to machines: The basketball doesn't fit in that box because it's too big. What is too big?

p. 118 Common sense in newborns: Paul Middlebrooks (host). "Liz Spelke: What Makes Us Special? (No. 48)" Brain Inspired, September 25, 2019. https://braininspired.co/podcast/48/

p. 119 "We're missing some basic insights." and p. 120 "I think that at some point…" Gary Marcus. Personal Interview, November 7, 2019 and Gary Marcus. "Deep Learning: A Critical Appraisal." January 2018. https://arxiv.org/abs/1801.00631

p. 120 "With artificial intelligence, we're summoning the demon." Elon Musk in Jaime Peraire (host) "One-on-one with Elon Musk." MIT AeroAstro Centennial Symposium, October 24, 2014. aeroastro.mit.edu

p. 120 The frog story was inspired by: Nick Bostrom. *Superintelligence.* Oxford University Press, 2014.

p. 122 "If we become better humans…" Ayanna Howard. *Sex, Race, and Robots: How to Be Human in the Age of AI.* Audible Originals, 2019

Inspiring | Educating | Creating | Entertaining

Brimming with creative inspiration, how-to projects, and useful information to enrich your everyday life, Quarto Knows is a favourite destination for those pursuing their interests and passions. Visit our site and dig deeper with our books into your area of interest: Quarto Creates, Quarto Cooks, Quarto Homes, Quarto Lives, Quarto Drives, Quarto Explores, Quarto Gifts, or Quarto Kids.

First published in 2021 by Frances Lincoln Children's Books, an imprint of The Quarto Group.
100 Cummings Center, Suite 265D, Beverly, MA 01915, USA.
T +1 978-282-9590 F +1 078-283-2742 www.QuartoKnows.com

A catalogue record for this book is available from the British Library.

ISBN 978-0-7112-5124-3
These artworks were created digitally.
Set in Aller, Neogrey, and Kelpt

Published by Katie Cotton
Designed by Myrto Dimitrakoulia
Edited by Lucy Brownridge and Katie Cotton
Production by Dawn Cameron

Manufactured in Guangdong, China TT072021

1 3 5 7 9 8 6 4 2